The complete book of cleaning

The complete book of cleaning

How to clean everything –
the right way
the lazy way
the green way

BARTY PHILLIPS

GUILD PUBLISHING
LONDON · NEW YORK · SYDNEY · TORONTO

Acknowledgements

Many thanks to all the individuals and companies who
have contributed to my fund of cleaning lore over the
years. In particular I would like to thank the listeners to
BBC Radio Sussex who have offered so many
suggestions, BBC TV's Bazaar who allowed me to
demonstrate several 'green' cleaning methods, Vic Allen
of *Green Magazine*, Frisky Lou who produced several
useful ideas from America, and my mother who first
told me how useful lemons could be.

© 1990 Barty Phillips

This edition published 1990
by Guild Publishing
by arrangement with
Judy Piatkus (Publishers) Ltd

CN 1134

Printed in Great Britain

Contents

Introduction

I clean, you clean, we all clean. In the last half century we have been aided and abetted by innumerable household chemicals to make things brighter, whiter, shinier and more hygienic with less effort.

Unfortunately, such thoroughness is often not good for the environment and not good for us. Caustics burn, phosphates pollute, perfumes and enzymes cause skin problems, most household chemicals are highly poisonous. And the worst of it is that we don't know what we are using half the time because there is no law which says labels have to carry a list of ingredients, as they do in food products.

This book does not dismiss chemical and proprietary cleaners out of hand – they have their uses in certain situations – but it does offer alternatives for those who prefer not to be polluting the environment or damaging their bodies. Both man-made and natural fibres require fairly specialised knowledge, but once you know what is needed they are not difficult to clean effectively, and indeed are often cleaned more easily with natural products than with chemicals.

Where appropriate this book offers three ways of cleaning:

1 The 'right' way, which is the most painstaking and thorough way, tried, tested and recommended by the experts but by no means necessarily the best way for everyday cleaning.

2 The 'lazy' way, which chooses short cuts where these make sense. Don't think that lazy is a derogatory term here. On the contrary anyone who can find ways of doing a satisfactory cleaning job using less effort or time merits a bonus mark for initiative.

3 The third way is the 'green' way or the environmentally friendly way. It is not always easy to define 'green'. Is it greener to put rubbish in plastic bags or paper carriers? Plastic is not considered to be a green material and usually it is not biodegradable. But the making of paper uses a precious (if renewable) natural resource.

And do you believe the manufacturers who tell you their washing powder is green because it contains no nitrates? You shouldn't because nitrates are not an ingredient of washing powders anyway. What we'd like to know is what IS in the product, not what isn't.

The green answer to cleaning is that it is fairly safe to use less of any cleaning agent than the manufacturers recommend and to try to stick to natural (which often means edible) cleaning agents such as vinegar, lemon juice and bicarbonate of soda. At least then you will be doing less damage. Happily the green way is often the lazy way as well, so you can combine the two with a good conscience.

Employing a cleaner

The ultimate lazy way for any type of cleaning is to hire someone else to do it, whether it's a firm of carpet cleaners, a window cleaner or someone to come in and help with the housework. The lazy alternatives given in this book are for people who simply don't have the time for anything else. Hiring a cleaner may be the answer if you don't have the time even for the 'lazy way'.

- When choosing a cleaner make sure you find somebody who comes with personal recommendations and who is good at the type of work you want done. There is no point in hiring a cook manqué if all you want is the lavatory cleaned thoroughly.
- Always, and particularly if you are hiring someone permanent, treat them well. Pay them the going rate for the area, no less and no more. Don't leave unnecessary chaos for them to cope with and then complain because you can't find things. If you find somebody you want and they have to (and are prepared to) travel some distance to get to you, pay a little extra to cover the fare.
- Don't give anyone your front door key unless or until you know them and have confidence in them.
- It's useful if you can be at home when they arrive or before they leave so that you build up a personal relationship. You'll get a more caring service that way.
- Don't feel forced to hire somebody twice a week or even once a week if all you want is a thorough going over once a fortnight.
- Make sure you both understand precisely what you want done. There are such things as 'treasures' who can read your mind and will do all tasks unbidden, but they are few and far between. You may find it helpful to refer your cleaner to this book.
- A useful alternative to hiring somebody permanently is to get a cleaning company to 'blitzclean' the house for a fairly steep sum, but then you won't be getting it done that often. Look in the Yellow Pages. Some cleaners only deal with contract cleaning jobs, others will cover domestic cleaning.

This book is intended to be an easy and quick reference guide whether you are dealing with everyday objects, something precious, something not encountered before or even an emergency. I hope most everyday cleaning situations are covered here and that you will find the solutions effective.

Throughout the text 'soap' refers to true soap and 'detergent' refers to synthetic detergents. The various A–Z sections will tell you how to deal with specific materials, specific stains and specific objects around the home. There is also a guide to cleaning products.

I hope you will enjoy using this book and treat it like a friend.

1
Laundering

Doing the washing is one of those thankless tasks that just has to be done. But with modern machines to wash, spin and even dry the laundry for you, there's no excuse for feeling a sense of martyrdom about it.

It isn't quite as simple as throwing everything dirty that you can lay your hands on into the machine and pressing the start button, however. Do this and you could open the machine door at the end of its programme to discover that your white tablecloth now matches your new crimson sweater which has itself shrunk beyond recognition.

THE CARE LABELS

Modern fabrics can be made of innumerable different yarns ranging from natural fibres like wool, cotton, linen and silk to man-made ones like viscose, acetate, nylon, polyester and so on, or mixtures of any of these. Each fibre has special requirements of its own and the only way to be certain of getting a good wash without damaging a garment is to follow the instructions on its care label. Most garments produced nowadays have such a label.

The care labels contain symbols and words that tell you if an item is washable and if so how it should be washed (ie whether to use a short, gentle cycle or a longer robust one) and at what temperature. They indicate if fabrics should be dry-cleaned only and if so whether they require a special dry-cleaning fluid. They also indicate if an item should be ironed and at what temperature. The chart on pages 6–7 explains the symbols.

Care labels

Washing

The wash tub number shows the most effective wash temperature.

New   Old

Normal wash cycle for cotton and other fabrics

Articles which can stand maximum conditions.

Reduced wash cycle for synthetics

Bar indicates medium washing conditions at temperature shown.

Minimum wash cycle for machine-washable wool and wool blends

Bar indicates a gentle wash.

Hand wash only

Do not machine wash

Bleaching

Chlorine bleach may be used

Tumble Drying

May be tumble dried

Use high heat setting

Use low heat setting

Ironing

Hot iron – cotton, linen, viscose

Warm iron – polyester mixtures, wool

Cool iron – acrylic, nylon, polyester

Dry-cleaning

A letter inside a circle indicates the types of dry-cleaning fluid that should be used.

Ⓟ Suitable to clean in perchloroethylene, white spirit, Solvent 113, Solvent 11.

Ⓟ As above with limitations as to heat, time and moisture. Caution in pre and post spotting.

Ⓕ Suitable to clean in white spirit and Solvent 113.

Ⓕ As above with limitations as to heat, time and moisture. Caution in pre and post spotting.

Ⓐ Normal textiles dry-cleanable in all solvents.

General

X A cross through any symbol means DO NOT.

Temperature guide

100°C   boil
 95°C   very hot (near boiling)
 60°C   hotter than the hand can bear
 50°C   hand hot
 40°C   pleasantly warm to the hand
 30°C   cool

Preparing the clothes

Whether washing by hand or machine, first prepare the items as follows.
- Do up zips and buttons, hooks and eyes, and poppers which may cause damage to other items in the wash.
- Sew on loose or missing buttons and mend any small tears.
- Remove debris from pockets.
- Brush off any loose dirt, especially dried mud. Dog and cat hairs can be removed with masking tape: press a strip on to the garment and pull it off – the hairs should come off with it.
- Tie up any ribbons, tapes, apron strings etc.
- If you are a loser of socks, use sock clips (available from hardware stores) to hold each pair together.

Sorting the clothes

Sort all items into groups of the same colour and the same wash code. If a garment has no care label (second-hand garments from jumble sales may pre-date the labelling regulations), wash it in a cool, minimum wash cycle in the machine or wash it by hand. Alternatively have it dry-cleaned.

Testing for colour fastness

Test new items for colour fastness before washing with other colours. Test a hidden area of the garment such as under the arm or at the back of the hem.
1   Dampen a cotton wool bud or tissue and leave it on the fabric for five minutes.
2   If any dye comes off on the cotton wool or tissue, wash the fabric separately or have it dry-cleaned.
3   If the colour has not run, it can be washed with white articles or other colours, provided you don't use the hottest wash.

Pre-wash treatments to loosen dirt

Removing stains

Look over each garment carefully and treat for stains if necessary. There are various products on the market which will loosen most stains before washing. You can use a spray or a bar of special soap which you rub on the mark. Use it on collars and cuffs and for stains such as make-up, sauce, wine, wax polishes, hair spray, medicines, egg, coffee, beetroot juice, suntan lotion etc. Or rub heavily with chalk which will absorb the oils and once the oil is removed the dirt will come off easily. See Chapter 3 for how to tackle specific stains.

Pre-washing

Very grubby work clothes, football shorts etc, should be given a pre-wash in the machine.

Soaking

A very effective pre-wash treatment is to soak clothes in detergent solution before washing. It's not necessary to use biological detergent – it's the soaking that gets the dirt out.
- For obstinate stains rub detergent in before soaking.
- Make sure the detergent is thoroughly dissolved before putting the clothes in or use liquid detergent.
- Don't soak coloureds and whites together.
- Don't soak silk, wool, leather, flame-retardant fabrics, non colour-fast fabrics or drip-dry fabrics.

Bleaching

Bleaching is a pre-wash treatment for removing stubborn stains from white fabrics (but see page 35). Liquid household bleaches are usually based on chlorine and they remove stains by adding oxygen. They should not be used on silk or wool. Chlorine bleaches are sold under various trade names.

Sodium perborate is also an oxidising bleach and is safe to use on silk and wool. It is in fact added to most washing powders.
- In care labels, a triangle containing the letters Cl indicates that the article can be safely treated with chlorine bleach. If the triangle has a cross through it chlorine bleach should not be used. The symbol ONLY refers to chlorine bleach, not other bleaches.
- To bleach a whole article in chlorine bleach use 10ml of bleach to 13 litres of cold water (2 teaspoons to 2½ gallons). Immerse the article for 10 to 15 minutes. Rinse thoroughly before washing as usual.
- Never use undiluted chlorine bleach.
- Never use chlorine bleach on silk, wool, rayon, drip-dry cottons or any article with a stain-resistant finish.

- A milder bleach is hydrogen peroxide (available from chemists) which can be used on silk and wool. Use in a solution of 1 part hydrogen peroxide to 8 parts water. Items can be soaked for up to 12 hours unless made of silk or wool which should never be soaked. Rinse thoroughly before washing as usual. See also page 36.

MACHINE WASHING – THE RIGHT WAY

- Load the machine correctly. Overloading will prevent the clothes moving around freely and they will not get clean.
- Select the correct programme (see pages 6–7).
- Don't use too much detergent – slightly less than the manufacturer's recommended amount should be sufficient. If you think there's some detergent left in the clothes after rinsing, put them through an extra rinse cycle. Left-over detergent in the fabric will attract dirt.
- Add fabric conditioner to the dispenser if liked (see below).
- Prevent coloured dyes running by putting salt in the wash or in the soaking water.
- Man-made fibres need a cold rinse cycle so that creases don't set. If you don't follow the care label at least see that you choose a suitable cycle.
- After a colour wash or after bleaching in the machine, put the machine through a rinse cycle so that the next load does not pick up any dye or bleach.
- After each wash, disconnect the machine from the electricity supply and wipe it down both inside and out using a clean, damp cloth.

Fabric conditioners

These can be added to the final rinse, whether machine or hand washing, to leave fabrics softer to the touch. Follow the manufacturer's instructions.

- They are particularly good for babies' clothes and nappies, sweaters, towels and other soft garments worn or used next to the skin.
- They make ironing easier and prevent the static electricity which can occur with nylon and other man-made fibres.

Spinning and drying

- Spinning or wringing will remove enough water from clothes so that you can hang them up to dry and they won't drip. A spinner capable of 800 or more revolutions a minute will get most clothes dry enough to iron.

- Twisting, wringing or spinning man-made fibres can cause creases in the fabric which are then impossible to remove, especially if the items are warm at the time. Anyway, man-made fibres are non-absorbent and so don't need a long spin.
- Don't overload the spin dryer and do take the clothes out as soon as the machine has stopped.
- If you can hang your clothes on an outside line they will smell fresh, have a soft texture and if the sun is out it will help to bleach them.
- A ceiling rack on a pulley is a good way of drying clothes indoors, if the ceiling is high enough.
- Heated drying racks and cabinets are another solution to the problem of drying washing indoors.
- Don't tumble-dry acrylics at a high setting.
- Never tumble-dry wool.
- Fold clothes (if completely dry) the moment you take them from the tumble-dryer – they should need little or no ironing.
- Tumble-drying sometimes causes static which can make clothes cling to the body. Ten minutes of cold tumble at the end of the drying cycle can reduce this effect.

Machine washing – the lazy way

- If you have no time for mending tears and securing loose buttons before washing, put garments loosely in a pillow case so they don't tear further in the wash.
- Use a shortish, coolish wash cycle for whites and 'fast' coloured garments together – unless the care label specifically warns to wash a garment separately.
- If you have no time to wash tights by hand, collect them up and wash them together in a loosely knotted pillow case, so they don't get tangled up.
- Leave out the soaking, bleaching etc, stage.

Machine washing – the green way

- Whenever possible use low temperature washes, economy washes and half load programmes, to save water and electricity.
- Don't use the machine if you only have two or three items – wash them by hand instead or wait until you have a full load.
- Use an environmentally 'friendly' powder.
- Most fabric conditioners have added perfumes to which many people are allergic. You can create your own fabric conditioner by

using a water softener in the rinse or even a water softener and half the normal amount of detergent in the wash. Or by using a non-perfumed hair conditioner in the rinse.

- A tumble-dryer is a very expensive if convenient way of drying clothes. A dry towel put in with the tumble-dry clothes will absorb moisture and reduce the drying time. Rolling wet clothes in a towel before tumble-drying will also remove a lot of moisture and save on electricity.

HAND WASHING – THE RIGHT WAY

Hand washing is preferable to machine washing for nylons, sweaters and delicate fabrics and garments.

- Before putting clothes in the water make sure the detergent or soap has dissolved completely.
- Soak clothes, except for woollens, for about two hours before hand washing to loosen the dirt.
- Squeeze clothes gently through the fingers. Don't rub hard. Wool should never be rubbed.
- Use a soft nail brush to loosen dirt round collar and cuffs but only if necessary.
- Natural fabrics, including wool, can be given a short spin after washing to get rid of excess water.
- Don't spin man-made fibres unless they are quite cold and then only for a very short time.

Hand washing – the lazy way

- There's no really lazy way of hand washing. Follow the instructions above.
- After hand washing some items can be rinsed in the machine using a suitable rinse cycle. Some machines have a special rinse and short spin programme for delicate hand-washed items.

Hand washing – the green way

- Use bar soap and some washing soda dissolved in hot water instead of detergent – this is very good for washing with.
- Add a tablespoon of white vinegar to the rinsing water to prevent soap scum.

SOME SPECIAL CASES

Blankets

Non-wool blankets can be washed in a machine, according to the fibre. It may be easier to use a large launderette machine and dryer; even if your machine will take it, drying will be a problem at home. Otherwise, take them to be dry-cleaned.

Crêpe fabrics

These may shrink after washing. Iron while still very damp and pull the fabric gently against the iron while you work.

Curtains

Wash curtains or have them cleaned at least once a year, following the manufacturer's care instructions. Test for colour fastness before washing (see page 8).
- Remove curtain hooks and weights before washing.
- Wash delicate fabrics by hand.
- If the curtains are lined, wash as for the 'weakest' fabric or it may shrink. Otherwise have them cleaned professionally.
- See page 25 for net curtains.

Drip-dry clothes

Don't use bleach on resin-finished cottons as it may combine with the finishing agent and then can't be rinsed out.

Duvets

Duvets filled with synthetic fibre can be washed at home or in a launderette machine. Feather-filled duvets can be washed at home, in a cool, short wash. Fluff them up while they are drying from time to time. Otherwise there are specialist firms who will clean feather-filled duvets.

Elastic and elasticised garments

Don't boil or wash in hot water. Don't wring or pull. Give a very short spin or roll in a towel to remove excess moisture.

Feather pillows

Immerse in a bath or tub of tepid water with 30g (1oz) washing soda crystals. Rinse through by lifting up and allowing to drain and then immersing again. Do this three or four times in fresh water without soda. You can use soapsuds for the wash and if you do, soften the first rinsing water with half a cup of white vinegar to ensure removal of all soap.

Knitted clothes

Wool should never be rubbed or moved around too much in water because of the scales on the fibre which felt up and shrink the fabric. Man-made fibre knits can stretch badly so wash them in the same way as wool, then pull into shape and dry flat. Use warm water and squeeze the garment in your hands – don't rub. Squeeze gently then roll up in a towel to get rid of excess moisture. Wool won't suffer from a short spin, but man-made fibres should only be spun if quite cold.

Lace

Store carefully and wash as seldom as possible. Soak in warm water then hand wash in hand-hot water.
- Don't wash lace of different colours together.
- Delicate lace should be pinned on to a linen-covered board and sponged gently with soapy water, then left to dry on the board.
- Don't use bleach on delicate lace.

Mildew

Treat while fresh.
- Wash thoroughly and dry in the sun.
- Or sponge with white vinegar before washing and soak in a solution of 5ml bleach to 1 litre of warm water (1 teaspoon to a quart).

Soft toys

Wash fairly often in warm suds and rinse thoroughly. Wash dark colours separately. Wrap in a towel to soak up excess moisture. Hang by the ears to dry.

Ties

Get professionally cleaned.

Towels which have gone musty

Add 3 tablespoons bicarbonate of soda to each litre (quart) of boiling water. Boil for 5 minutes, then launder as usual.

Shower curtains

Wash in cool cycle of machine adding a little detergent and bleach. Put two old white bath towels in with the wash. Add one cup of white vinegar to the rinsing water. Do not spin dry. See also page 26.

White cotton socks

Add a slice of lemon to the water and boil them for five minutes to restore whiteness.

STARCHING

Starch stiffens limp fabrics but also helps to keep out dirt, and most fabrics wear better when starched. The soft gloss finish it gives cottons holds down the fine surface hairs and fills the gaps between fibres where dust and dirt collect. Too much starch, however, can cause dryness and cracking of the fabric.

Instant starch

This is a powder soluble in cold or warm water. Make up a solution according to the packet instructions. Dip the garment in the starch solution after the last rinse.

Powder starch

This type of starch has to be mixed up like mustard: first cream with cold water and then mix with boiling water, then dilute for dipping the clothes in. It is good for articles that need to be very stiff but it's quite a tedious job and extravagant in its use of water, so it's not very practical unless you have a great many things which need starching.

Spray starch

This is water soluble and can be sprayed on fabrics just before ironing. It's the most convenient type of starch to use.

IRONING – THE RIGHT WAY

- Leave the iron to warm up for five minutes after you've switched it on. This will give the thermostat time to settle and the sole plate time to heat up evenly.
- Start with the items that need the coolest setting, such as silk and acetate, and increase the heat as you get to the more robust cottons and linens. Always follow the care label.
- Pull napkins and hankies etc into shape before you iron them.
- Tack pleats in place before ironing.
- Press embossed cottons on the wrong side.
- Very dry creased fabric should be generously splashed with water and rolled up for a couple of hours before ironing to let the moisture spread through the fibres.
- A garden spray bottle is useful for spraying moisture on to dry fabrics if you have not got a steam iron.

Ironing a shirt

1   Iron the collar, starting at the points and working towards the back.
2   Iron the cuffs.
3   Iron the sleeves, starting at the under-arm seams. Run the point of the iron into the gathers at the cuff and work up towards the shoulder.
4   Iron one front and work round to the other front. Hang the shirt to air before folding.
5   Fold sides to middle, fold arms back. Fold bottom to top, arms inside.

Ironing trousers

1   Iron pockets.
2   Fit the top part of the trousers over the end of the ironing board and iron.
3   Fold trousers lengthways, seams to the middle, creases at the outside edges. Iron the inside and then outside of the leg.
4   Turn trousers over and iron the other leg in the same way.

Ironing sheets

Fold the sheets in four lengthways. Iron the outside surfaces, then turn the folds inwards and iron again.

Ironing – the lazy way

- Fold T-shirts and sweat shirts when still slightly damp, smooth flat and dry in a warm place. They won't need ironing at all.
- Pull damp sheets hard at each corner (you need two people for this), fold, smooth and dry on a warm surface or in the airing cupboard. They shouldn't need ironing.
- Putting trousers in a trouser press is a good alternative to ironing them.
- Buy items made of easy-care drip-dry fabrics that don't need ironing.
- Iron only the parts that will be seen (e.g. the top of a sheet).

Ironing – the green way

- The lazy way is also the green way as you use up less energy. See above.

PRESSING

Pressing is an ironing technique used on tweed suits, wool and other things which are too heavy to iron satisfactorily or which might singe or go shiny if ironed. Use a hot iron and a clean, damp, lint-free cloth – a tea towel works well or a bit of old but clean cotton sheet.

1 Place the garment on the ironing board with the damp cloth on top.
2 Press the iron down then lift it and press it again. Don't slide it over the cloth. Continue until the cloth is dry and the garment flat. If necessary damp the cloth again at intervals.
3 Air the clothes well after pressing and before hanging them in a wardrobe.

• If you have a steam iron you can press very lightweight fabrics under a dry cloth.
• When pressing pleats, tack them in place first, EXACTLY on the crease line.

2
A-Z of fabrics and their care

Every fibre whether natural or man-made has characteristics which require special treatment. For instance viscose becomes weak while it is in water so should not be soaked for too long; many synthetics will acquire permanent creases if they get too hot when wet and wool shouldn't be rubbed in water or it will shrink.

The following is a list of the most commonly used fabrics and fibres and is intended as a quick reference guide on how to care for them.

Acetate
Man-made cellulose acetate fibre usually of wood pulp. Quite silk-like in appearance, colour fast, won't shrink.
- Warm wash, gentle action, cold rinse.
- Spin only if the care label says so. Do not wring or twist.
- Drip-dry or roll in a towel to remove excess moisture.
- Iron while still damp with a cool iron.
- Knitted acetates should be given a cold rinse and short spin.
- Don't use acetic acid, acetone, alcohol or similar chemicals for stain removal or the fabric will dissolve.

Acrylic
By-products of oil refining. Soft, warm, durable and mildew-resistant. Won't shrink.
- Warm wash, cold rinse, short spin.
- Rinse pleated garments and drip-dry.
- Pull heavy knitwear into shape and dry flat on a towel.
- Pile fabrics may be brushed lightly with a soft brush when dry.
- Some garments need to be ironed lightly with a cool iron once the garment is dry.

Angora

Fluffy rabbit wool used for jumpers, hats, scarves etc. Very soft with characteristic white hairs. Sometimes mixed with nylon.
- Hand wash and treat as for wool.

Astrakhan

Lamb's skin or imitation lamb's skin.
- Treat as sheepskin: dry-clean or shampoo or wash as for wool.
- No need to iron.

Bonded fibres

Off-white, crush resistant, porous, water-repellent and light. Used for interlinings.
- Warm wash; don't rub.
- Roll loosely in a towel to absorb moisture.
- Don't spin or wring.

Braid

Used to decorate some garments.
- Dry-clean only. Sprinkle with bicarbonate of soda, leave, then brush off with a fine wire brush.
- Or make a paste of methylated spirit and French chalk to remove tarnish.
- Or use a mixture of cream of tartar and dry bread, apply when dry and brush lightly with a clean, soft brush.

Brocade

May be acetate, cotton, silk, viscose or a mixture.
- Dry-clean only. Too heavy to handle when wet.

Broderie anglaise

Openwork embroidered fabric of white cotton or cotton/polyester.
- Wash as for cotton, but make sure other garments have no hooks to catch in the embroidery.

Buckram

Cotton stiffening fabric treated with size.
- Dry-clean only.

Calico

Medium weight cotton.
- Wash as for cotton.
- Put splash of white spirit into the first wash of unbleached calico to remove the starch and whiten the fabric.

Cambric

Handkerchief cotton.
• Wash as for cotton.

Camel hair

Expensive, soft, warm brown wool.
• Dry-clean only.

Candlewick

Tufted fabric of nylon, polyester, rayon, triacetate or cotton.
• Wash as for fibre concerned.

Canvas or duck

Very stiff cotton used for tents and yacht sails, handbags and shoes.
• Scrub with a block of soap and a scrubbing brush then pour buckets of water over it to rinse.

Cashmere

Light, soft wool from the Kashmir goat. Scarce and expensive.
• Wash as for wool.

Cavalry twill

Tough, heavy, woven fabric used for trousers, riding breeches etc. Can be wool, cotton or man-made fibres.
• Dry-clean unless label says wash.

Chenille

Fabric with soft, velvety pile. May be cotton, rayon, wool or silk.
• Wash or dry-clean according to fibre.

Chiffon

Sheer fabric with soft rippled finish. May be silk, rayon or other man-made fibres.
• Wash as for fibre concerned.
• Don't wring.
• When almost dry, iron gently and patiently with cool iron. Stretch garment gently in all directions then into its correct shape as you iron.

Chintz

Cotton fabric with a shiny side.
• Dry-clean.
• If you DO wash use starch or a plastic stiffener unless the glaze is permanent.

Ciré
Usually nylon-treated fabric used in showerproof garments.
- Sponge, rather than wash, so as not to remove the dressing. Drip-dry and press with a cool iron and a cloth.

Corduroy
Also needle cord and elephant cord. Can be cotton, cotton/viscose or cotton/polyester.
- Wash as for the more delicate fibre.
- Occasionally smooth the pile as it dries and shake it from time to time. Should then need no ironing.
- If you must iron, press gently while still damp on the wrong side with several thicknesses of folded material between the garment and the iron.

Cotton
Cotton fabrics are absorbent and tough, washable and hang well.
- Wash white cotton in hot or boiling water.
- Test coloured cottons for fastness. Safest to wash reds with reds, blues with blues and so on, anyway.
- Always follow the care label instructions especially for delicate cottons such as voile, organdie or drip-dry and stain-repellent fabrics.

Crêpe
Fabric with wrinkled, crinkled surface.
- Wash in hand-hot water. Roll in a towel to absorb excess moisture.
- Iron on the wrong side with warm iron while still damp or use steam iron.

Damask
Woven patterned fabric, can be cotton, silk, wool, viscose or a mixture.
- Treat as for weakest fibre. See care label.

Denim
Heavy cotton, also available in rayon/cotton mixture.
- Wash as for weakest fibre.
- Denim will shrink slightly unless pre-shrunk.

Dralon
Brand name for an acrylic fibre.

Elastomers

Fibres mostly based on polyurethane which have the elasticity of rubber.
- Follow the care label or hand wash in warm water or give gentle machine wash.
- Rinse, short spin or roll in a towel; drip-dry.
- Don't iron.

Faille

Fine ribbed fabric. May be silk, cotton or man-made fibres.
- Treat as for fibre concerned.

Felt

Matted woollen material. Shrinks easily.
- Don't wash.
- To clean at home, make a paste with white spirit and French chalk. Rub well in and let it dry, then brush it off.

Flannel

See wool.

Flannelette

Heavyish weight brushed cotton fabric used for sheets and winter nighties.
- Wash as for cotton.

Flock Fabric

Fabric with a velvet pile pattern.
- Wash in hand-hot suds.
- Don't spin or wring. Roll in towel to remove moisture.
- Iron on wrong side with a warm iron or drip-dry.

Foulard

Usually acetate, may be silk.
- Wash according to fibre.

Fur Fabric

May be of nylon, viscose, cotton, acrylic or polyester.
- Cotton and viscose should be dry-cleaned.
- Others may be washed according to fibre or care label instructions. If in doubt, wash as nylon.
- Or lightly sponge fur fabric with warm detergent solution, sponge, rinse and dry with a towel.

Gabardine

Strong woven fabric twilled with diagonal ribs. Can be of cotton, worsted or blends of those and man-made fibres.
* Dry-clean.

Georgette

Delicate, sheer fabric a bit like crêpe. Can be of wool, cotton, silk or man-made fibres.
* If silk or wool, get garment professionally cleaned.
* Wash man-made fabrics according to weakest fibre or follow the care label.
* Test for colour fastness (see page 8).

Gingham

See Cotton.

Glass Fibre

Fine glass filaments.
* Handle with care; wear rubber gloves.
* Do not machine wash, spin, wring, dry-clean or iron.
* Do not wash with other garments.
* Hand wash by gently moving fabric round in the suds.
* Don't use bleach.
* Rinse in warm water, drip-dry, pull hem straight.
* Rinse sink out well afterwards to remove any slivers of glass.

Grosgrain

Finely ribbed fabric, may be from various fibres.
* Wash or dry-clean according to fibre or the care label.

Jersey

Stretchy knitted fabric in stockinette stitch. Can be of wool, silk, cotton, nylon or other man-made fibres.
* Wash or dry-clean according to the care label.
* No care label? Get the garment dry-cleaned.

Kapok

From seed pods of the kapok tree. Waterproof, light, fluffy, resilient. Used for stuffing mattresses and cushions. Liable to go lumpy in the wash.
* Dry-clean only.

Lace

Can be cotton, polyester, nylon or a mixture.
- Wash according to fibre. Use a soap or detergent specially formulated for delicate fabrics.
- Old lace should be put in a pillow case to be washed.
- Curtain lace should be washed in hot suds. If cotton, boil from time to time.
- Pull into shape while drying.
- Iron with a hot iron on the wrong side.
- For delicate hand-made lace see page 14.

Lamé

See Metallic yarns.

Lawn

Fine fabric of cotton, polyester/cotton or viscose/cotton blends.
- Hand wash or give the article a very short, gentle machine wash.
- Use hand-hot water, rinse thoroughly and wring or spin.

Leather gloves

- Wash the gloves while on your hands in warm water and soap-flakes.
- Pale coloured gloves should be washed each time they are worn.
- Leave some soap in the gloves after washing.
- Dry over wooden or wire hands or, if you haven't got any, over a bottle.
- When they are dry, rub the leather between your fingers to soften it.

Leather shoes

- Wet leather shoes should be stuffed with newspaper and dried away from direct heat. A little castor oil rubbed into the uppers and soles after they have dried will soften them and recondition the leather.
- Polish leather shoes frequently (see page 121).

Linen

Woven from fibres of the flax plant. Similar to cotton but with a better texture and longer life.
- Hot wash, rinse thoroughly, spin dry.
- Iron on the wrong side with hot iron while still damp unless you have an iron with spray steam for bad creases.

Metallic yarns

Non-tarnishable aluminium threads coated with plastic and woven with other yarns.
- Dry-clean only.

Milium

A metal-finished fabric which is a very good insulator.
- Dry-clean.

Modacrylic

Modified acrylic, similar to acrylic but not so strong.
- Wash in warm water and detergent, rinse well.
- Drip-dry.
- If necessary iron with a cool iron.

Mohair

See Wool.

Moiré

See Silk.

Mungo

See Wool.

Muslin

Thin loosely woven cotton.
- Wash in warm water, rinse well.
- Iron while damp with warm iron. Starch.

Net

Fine mesh material, can be of cotton, nylon, polyester etc. Cotton net may shrink when washed for the first time.
- Curtain nets should be washed often; once really dirty it's impossible to get them clean.
- Shake first, then rinse in cold water. Wash in hot water. Wash twice if necessary.
- Do not rub, twist or wring, just squeeze suds gently through fabric.
- If curtains have gone grey, wash in a proprietary curtain whitener then try white nylon dyes.
- As a last resort, try soaking in biological detergent.
- Net on dresses should be hand-washed in warm soap-flakes. Rinse, drip-dry and iron with a warm iron while still a little damp.

Nylon

Strong, elastic, does not lose its strength when wet, lightweight, absorbs little moisture, flame resistant, resistant to most oils and chemicals, moths and moulds.

- Wash in hand-hot water, cold rinse, short spin, drip-dry. It's basic state is grey and the white pigment will come out if you use hot water. Supermarkets sell nylon whiteners which you can try in the rinsing water.
- Don't use bleach except on mildewed shower curtains, which can be sponged with a weak mixture of chlorine bleach (or see page 76). More drastically, use a fungicide, available in plastic sachets from hardware shops.
- Don't expose nylon to direct heat or sunlight.
- Shouldn't need ironing. If it does, use a warmish setting when almost dry. Never iron pleated nylon.
- Dip pleated garments up and down in the suds.
- Wash pleated and delicate garments every time you use them; once really dirty the dirt won't come out.
- If sent for dry-cleaning, mark clearly 'Nylon'.
- Nylon fur with an interlining should not be washed but given a wet shampoo. Mix some liquid detergent in warm water and sponge the lather into the fur only. Treat a small patch at a time and don't wet the lining or interlining. Rinse with a clean, not-too-wet sponge and pat dry with a towel. Or use a dry shampoo.

Organdie

Permanently stiffened delicate fabric, can be cotton or nylon.

- Squeeze gently in hand-hot water and mild detergent, rinse well.
- Wring or spin and hang to dry.
- Iron on the right side while still damp.
- Limp organdie can be rinsed in a litre of warm water with 50g borax (one tablespoon to a quart).
- Nylon organdie should be washed as nylon.

Organza

Sort of stiffened chiffon, may be silk or various fibres.

- Wash according to fibre and handle with care.

Polyester

From by-products of petrol refining. Very strong whether wet or dry. High resistance to abrasion, sheer, lightweight. Won't shrink or stretch. Resistant to moths and mildew. Often combined with cotton.
• Hand or machine wash, cold rinse, normal spin. Can be tumble-dried.
• Do not boil.
• Loosen bad stains by impregnating them with concentrated detergent, leaving for 15 minutes then laundering as usual.
• Wash pleated garments by hand and hang to drip-dry.

Poplin

Can be cotton, viscose, silk or wool.
• Wash as for relevant fibre.

PVC

Strong man-made plastic material.
• Hand-wash only, drip-dry only. Do not iron.

Rayon

See Viscose.

Repp

Heavy woven fabric, can be cotton or mixture of cotton and man-made fibres.
• Treat as for weakest fibre. See care label.

Sateen

Satin-like fabric, may be cotton or viscose.
• Treat as for weakest fibre.

Satin

Smooth, slippery material with short nap. Can be silk, cotton, polyester, nylon or acetate.
• Wash lightweight satins according to fibre. Press on wrong side while still damp, until completely dry.
• Acetate satin should be ironed on the wrong side with a cool iron while evenly damp. Do not sprinkle with water or it will spot.
• Dry-clean heavier furnishing satins.

Seersucker

Crinkled lightweight fabric, can be cotton, silk, nylon or polyester.
• Wash as for the fibre.
• Needs no ironing.

Serge

Suiting fabric in worsted or blends of wool and viscose or other fibres.
- Dry-clean or wash quickly in warm water, squeeze out water and dry away from direct heat.
- Press under a damp cloth with a warm iron.

Shantung

Chinese silk with slubs. May also be acetate or nylon.
- Wash as appropriate for the fibre.

Sharkskin

Smooth woven or knitted fabric, may be cotton or more usually acetate.
- Wash as for the fibre.
- May show watermarks if ironed over damp patches so dry evenly and don't iron until almost dry.

Sheepskin

Wool from sheep, or may be acrylic.
- Machine wash in the wool programme.
- Can be shampooed in hand-hot water with a mild detergent. Rinse in warm water, squeeze out moisture and dry away from direct heat.
- Or take to a specialist cleaner.

Silk

Silk does not conduct heat so keeps in the heat of the body and is warm to wear. It is also strong, resilient, elastic and wrinkle resistant. Sunlight and perspiration can weaken it.
- Silk taffetas and brocades should be dry-cleaned.
- Wash garments every time you wear them or perspiration stains may be impossible to remove and weaken the fabric.
- Other stains should be removed professionally, but tell the cleaner what the stain is.
- Don't soak in biological detergent.
- Iron while still damp with a cool iron or a steam iron.
- Bleach white silk with a solution of hydrogen peroxide or sodium perborate type bleaches.
- Silk stockings last longer if soaked in clean, cold water before you wear them. After wearing wash in lukewarm water and detergent. Squeeze gently, don't rub.

- If you wash coloured silks immerse the garments in a solution of 10ml strong acetic acid (or vinegar) to 3 litres water (2 teaspoons to 6 pints) after the final rinse. Leave for a few minutes then dry without rinsing. This is to ensure the colours won't be affected by any alkali in the washing detergent.
- Don't rub silk while it is wet or the filaments break up and produce a white, chalky effect.

Taffeta

Plain, shiny, close-woven fabric, may be of silk, wool, acetate, viscose, polyester or nylon.
- Most taffetas should be dry-cleaned. Nylon may be washed.

Terylene

See Polyester.

Ticking

Striped closely-woven cotton material used to cover mattresses and pillows and to keep the feathers in.
- Wash as for cotton.
- When dry, rub the inside with beeswax as an extra barrier for the feathers.

Triacetate

A development of cellulose acetate fibres, made from wood pulp and cotton. Can be embossed or permanently pleated, resists dirt and creasing, won't shrink or stretch, can be woven or knitted and dries quickly. Often blended with other fibres.
- Hand-wash in warm water and detergent, swirl gently but don't squeeze. Drip-dry.
- If machine washing give short, warm wash with cold rinse and short spin.
- If necessary use a cool iron.
- Triacetate can be dry-cleaned with perchloroethylene. Care label should have a 'P' symbol.
- Don't use acetone, acetic acid or alcohol as stain removers or the fabric will dissolve.

Tricot

Jersey fabric made of viscose, nylon or polyester.
- Wash as appropriate for fibre.

Tulle

Fine net of cotton, viscose, nylon or other fibres.
- Wash as for fibre.
- If the net becomes limp, dip cotton tulle in weak starch; nylon and rayon tulle in a gum arabic solution.

Tweed

Heavy twilled woollen fabric, sometimes also polyester or acrylic.
- Dry-clean woollen tweeds.
- Wash according to fibre.

Velour

Fabric with a heavy pile, usually acrylic but may be other man-made fibres or cotton or silk.
- Dry-clean.

Velvet

Pile fabric of silk, cotton, wool, viscose, nylon etc. Many are uncrushable, spot-proof and easily washed.
- Wash according to fibre.
- Shake occasionally while drying and smooth the pile with a soft cloth or a velvet brush.
- Or dry-clean.

Vicuna

See Wool.

Viscose

Man-made fibre of wood pulp. Weak when wet, strong when dry. Can look like silk, linen, wool or cotton but should be treated more gently.
- Hand-wash frequently in warm water.
- Don't twist, wring or pull while washing.
- Iron with steam iron or while still damp.
- Iron shiny fabrics on the right side, matt fabrics on the wrong side.

Viyella

Brand name for a woven cotton and wool fabric.
- Wash gently by hand in hot water.
- Iron on the wrong side while still damp.

Voile

Sheer woven material may be of cotton, viscose, nylon or polyester.
- Wash as appropriate for fibre.

Winceyette

Brushed material similar to flanelette but lighter. May be cotton or cotton and wool or viscose blends.
- Wash as for wool or viscose.

Wool

Natural fibre from the coats of sheep, lambs and goats or camels. Special sorts of wool are made from the alpaca, llama, vicuna, camel, goat and rabbit. Wool has a coating of scales which work against each other if the wool is rubbed while wet and this causes the fibres to shrink and 'felt'. Wool also stretches when wet (but will never 'unfelt'). Wool absorbs moisture, is resilient, elastic and resists wrinkling.

- Hand wash unless the care label says it's machine washable. Squeeze the garment gently, never rub, twist or wring. Use a soapless detergent or a specially formulated wool detergent for use in cold water.
- A very short spin will get rid of excess moisure without spoiling the garment. Never tumble-dry wool.
- Lay the garment flat on a towel and pull gently into correct shape, then leave to dry.
- Yellowed white wool can be soaked in a solution of 1 part hydrogen peroxide to 10 parts water. Rinse in warm water.
- Wash oiled wool in warm water using thoroughly dissolved soap-flakes (not detergent which will remove the oil) or a special wool wash liquid. You can't re-oil wool so treat it gently.

3
Stain removal
at home

This chapter deals with how to tackle stains on fabrics using one of the four basic stain removing techniques: absorbing, flushing through, using solvents or bleaching. Understanding the reason for the different techniques involved enables you to work out for yourself how to treat stains and fabrics.

HOME STAIN REMOVAL KIT

Have an emergency stain removal kit in the home so that you can deal with stains straightaway. This gives the best chance of success.

Keep everything well labelled and out of the reach of children. A well-stocked emergency kit should contain the following items:

- Squirter bottle for spraying cold water
- White tissues, small sponges and white, absorbent cotton wool
- Salt
- Medicine dropper for application of powerful solvents (don't *store* solvent in it though)
- Fuller's earth, bran, French chalk or talcum powder
- Bicarbonate of soda
- Household bleach (chlorine bleach)
- Hydrogen peroxide
- Sodium perborate
- Household ammonia
- Amyl acetate (or non-oily nail varnish remover)
- Proprietary dry-cleaning solvent
- White spirit
- White vinegar (acetic acid)
- Lemon juice (citric acid)

- Margarine, glycerine
- An ironing board makes a good work bench.

ABSORBING

Use this for wet things spilled on fabric and carpets before the stain dries, and also to get rid of greasy particles in fur and other unwashable fabrics. There are various suitable absorbents:

Salt

This will absorb urine, fruit juice and red wine. Pour a generous amount on to carpet, tablecloth etc and leave for several hours to soak up the liquid. Then vacuum or shake out and dry-clean, launder or shampoo (carpets and rugs).

Tissues

Use white tissues to absorb the liquid if you have no salt. Place several on to the stain and tread on them gently. Don't rub. When the tissues become saturated, remove them and apply fresh ones.

Bran, fuller's earth, French chalk and talcum powder

All of these will absorb grit and dirt from fur, felt etc, in the same way that dry shampoos clean hair. Shake on to the garment. Leave for 12 hours or so. Brush out gently but thoroughly.

FLUSHING THROUGH – THE RIGHT WAY

Use this method for liquids, fruit juices, wine and non-greasy stains on washable fabrics. Cold water is still one of the best stain removers.
- Use cold water or cold water and liquid detergent for non-greasy stains.

1   Lay the fabric face down on an absorbent pad of paper tissue or cotton wool or white, lint-free cloth. This will help to draw out the stain.

2   Use a spray bottle to force water through just the stain. Some stains may respond to neat liquid detergent being squirted through the fabric and left for a little while before flushing out.

3   When the stain is dissolved, flush with water from well outside the stained area, working towards the centre, using a squeezy bottle with a fine spray or a medicine dropper.

4   Rinse thoroughly and wash as usual.

- Don't use water on dyed wild silk, or moiré patterns which show up on only the right side of the fabric.

Flushing through – the lazy way

- Leave the stained part of the garment soaking in cold water or water and detergent for an hour or two then rinse thoroughly before laundering as usual. Don't try this lazy way on special clothes or delicate fabrics.

Flushing through – the green way

- If soaking items (see The Lazy Way, above), don't use enzyme detergents. They don't really help anyway.
- Use as little of all household detergents and solvents as you can.
- Use liquid detergents without phosphates or perfumes.
- Use *very* dilute bleach and leave it to work for longer than usual.
- Soda water will flush out red wine if you catch it straight away. If using on a carpet, mop up well between applications so as not to get the carpet too wet.

USING SOLVENT – THE RIGHT WAY

Use on grease, oil or stains which have a greasy base, such as milk, cream, sauce, lipstick etc.

The most common solvents, sold as spot removers under various trade names, are trichloroethane and perchloroethylene. Proprietary stain removers may be in liquid, aerosol or paste form. Other useful solvents are white spirit, surgical spirit or acetone (not for use on acetate fabrics).

- Always follow the manufacturers' instructions where they exist. Many solvents are flammable and/or poisonous, so use them with care.
- Don't use solvents near a naked flame or in a confined space.

1   Scrape off as much of any solid matter as you can without damaging the fabric. A blunt knife is a useful tool and usually to hand.

2   Put a white cloth or paper tissue under the stain to prevent it being transferred to another part of the garment.

3   Soak another cloth in solvent and dab in a circle, starting outside the stain and working towards the centre.

4   Rinse thoroughly and wash according to the care label or, if the garment is not washable, air it well or dry gently with a warm hair dryer.

Using solvents – the lazy way

There's no lazy way to remove these kinds of stains – the job must be done at once and with patience. If you can't be bothered or don't feel confident, take the garment to a dry-cleaner as soon as possible.

Using solvents – the green way

- Don't use aerosols.
- Use margarine, glycerine or white vaseline to soften tar and oil before laundering.
- Use white vinegar instead of a proprietary solvent.
- If you do use solvents, don't pour them down the drain. Instead absorb them with a piece of old rag and put them with the rubbish.

BLEACHING STAINS – THE RIGHT WAY

Use this treatment for residual stains which remain after you have used other techniques. Use only on white fabrics or very diluted and for a short time on coloureds. See general instructions for bleaching on page 9.

- Before using bleach on coloured fabrics always test a small piece of the fabric where it can't be seen (inside the hem or a seam) for colour fastness (see page 8).

For small stains

1 Mix 10ml household bleach with 800ml cold water (2 teaspoons to 1½ pints).
2 Put a clean cloth or a wad of tissue under the fabric exactly below the stain and dab the stain with another cloth moistened with the diluted bleach solution.
3 Rinse the garment thoroughly then wash or dry-clean as usual.
NOTE: don't splash bleach on the clothes you are wearing and make sure there's none left in garments after rinsing that could affect other clothes in the wash.

Bleaching whole garments

1 Use 10ml bleach to 13 litres water (2 teaspoons to 2½ gallons). Immerse article for 10 to 15 minutes.
2 Rinse thoroughly before washing as usual.
- Dygon is a proprietary product which will remove most tea, coffee, wine, fruit and other stains from white fabrics. Follow the instructions on the pack. Don't remove stains from coloured fabrics in this way unless they are guaranteed colour-fast. Dygon will bleach grey linens, cottons, towels etc.

Bleaching stains – the lazy way

Use slightly more bleach than recommended and it will take slightly less time to work.

NOTE: check garment frequently and don't leave in the stronger solution too long or the fabric will suffer. Use stronger solution bleach only on white articles.

Bleaching stains – the greener way

Use hydrogen peroxide or sodium perborate which are milder than chlorine bleach (see below). Both can be used safely on wool and silk.

Using hydrogen peroxide

- Use 1 part peroxide to 8 parts water for bleaching. Items can be soaked for up to 12 hours, but don't soak silk or wool. Before using on rayons and nylons test for colour fastness (see page 8).
- For stubborn stains apply the hydrogen peroxide and water solution with a medicine dropper or a spray bottle directly on to the stain, putting a pad of tissue underneath. Keep adding more bleach solution until the stain disappears. Don't pour peroxide back into the bottle because it is very susceptible to impurities.

Using sodium perborate

- Dissolve 1 to 2 tablespoons of sodium perborate crystals in 600ml (1 pint) water as hot as the material will allow. Soak for several hours because this is a slow working bleach, unless the material is wool or silk in which case squeeze the bleach through the material gently – don't soak. If the fabric becomes yellowed by the solution, sponge it well with white vinegar and then rinse it.
- Non-washable materials may be sprinkled with sodium perborate and covered with a cotton-wool pad dampened with water. Use hot water if you can, or lukewarm water on heat-sensitive fabrics. Keep the pad damp until the stain has disappeared – this may take several hours.

The sun

Alternatively leave newly washed clothes out in the sun to dry as the sun acts as a bleach.

SOME BASIC STAIN REMOVAL RULES

- Deal with a stain as soon as possible, AT ONCE if you can.
- If you are not sure what created a stain, or what the fabric content of the garment is, take the garment to a professional cleaner.
- Scrape off any solid matter at once with a blunt knife or, if it has dried, loosen it with a solvent or pat it with a stiff bristle brush (don't use a brushing action).
- Dress fabrics with special surfaces like taffeta, velvet or satin should always be cleaned professionally or you may ruin the surface effect.
- Hold the fabric stain-down so the stain will go out the way it came in rather than trying to push it right through the fabric.
- Keep a pad of clean, white tissue or cotton material underneath the stained area to absorb stain remover and stain.
- Don't apply heat to the fabric in any form before tackling a stain. Many foods contain albumen or similar protein which is 'fixed' by heat. So don't, for instance, wash the garment in hot water or hold it over the steam from a kettle.
- Do test any stain remover on a hidden piece of garment first – the inside hem for instance, or an inside seam. Some treatments may make the colours run or fade, and some may damage the fibres.
- Don't try to remove the last traces of stubborn stains. It's often better to wear the thing with a residual stain barely showing than risk ruining the fabric by applying too much solvent or over-zealous rubbing.
- Dissolve any residual stain in a suitable fluid (water, water and detergent, or solvent).
- Upholstery and carpets must be sponged and dabbed dry alternately so they don't get too wet. Don't let the liquid get into any padding or backing, where it may do irreparable damage. (See pages 83–5 and 102–5).
- When the stain has dissolved, start flushing with water or solvent well outside the stained area, moving round and working towards the centre. A plastic bottle with a fine spray nozzle is good for this.
- If you have used solvent, blot up any excess with a clean, dry cloth or sponge and drive off any remaining with a stream of warm air from a hair dryer, using a circular motion, as when cleaning.
- If you used bleach or detergent, finish by rinsing thoroughly and washing the garment as usual.
- Always rinse the area well between types of treatment if the first attempt doesn't work.
- Never mix solvents before use.

Testing for colour fastness

Some dyes only remain fixed for a limited time so test all fabrics for colour fastness each time you treat the garment in a new way, especially if you think it will have to spend a long time in contact with the stain removal agent.

1   Make up the cleaning solution in the proportion you intend to use it.
2   Apply it to a hidden piece of the garment.
3   Put the treated area between two pieces of clean white fabric or tissue and press with a warm iron.
4   If any colour has been transferred to the white fabric or tissue then it is not colour fast and should be dealt with by a professional.

Final touches

Sometimes powdery particles stay trapped between the fibres after the rest of the stain has dissolved and been flushed away. Don't scrape at these with your fingernail. Deal with them by applying neat liquid detergent and gently working the fabric between your fingers. Then rinse with water three or four times otherwise any residual detergent will attract dirt again.

• Don't use spirits or solvents on viscose, triacetate or rain-proofed fabrics.
• BE PATIENT: gentle dabbing and rinsing over a long period will work in the end where brisk rubbing would ruin the cloth.

Spot cleaning check list

1   Act fast.
2   Scrape off solids.
3   Absorb liquids.
4   Treat the stain with a suitable liquid (water, water and detergent or solvent).
5   Treat any residual stain with bleach (fabric permitting).

4
A-Z of stains

The advice in this chapter relates to stains on fabrics and carpets and is based on the basic rules and techniques in Chapter 3.

It is possible to buy a range of proprietary products formulated for specific stains. Some of these are very effective, others less so. They are all relatively expensive and involve the use of chemicals. If you are looking for cheaper or greener stain removers or you have no relevant proprietary treatment to hand, here are some tried and tested alternative methods for removing the various types of stains.

Acids

Flush at once with cold water. Acids do not necessarily stain fabrics but they are quite likely to destroy them. Even a weak acid will damage fibres, especially cotton, linen, nylon, viscose and coloured materials. When flushed, neutralise any acid left with household ammonia (diluted as directed on the bottle) or bicarbonate of soda dissolved in a little water. Rinse well.

Adhesives

If you get any proprietary adhesive where you did not intend to, check the label or packaging for advice. The manufacturers will often have advice if you ring them or write to them. Here are some specific types of glue and how to deal with them. Remember that some modern glues cannot be removed once they have dried.

Animal and fish glues Usually soluble in cold water. If not, wet the stain with cold water anyway, treat with household ammonia and rinse. If the stain is still there, wet it again, apply liquid detergent and rinse.

Household adhesives and model aircraft cement These are cellulose-based. Use non-oily nail varnish remover or acetone on most fabrics except acetate fabrics. (Chemically pure amyl acetate won't damage such fabrics, but as the adhesive has acetone in it the fabric will have been damaged anyway.)

Cyanoacrylates ('superglues') These 'bond in seconds' and are quite difficult to use. If fingers, eyelids etc, get stuck together, don't panic. The glue is activated by moisture and soluble in moisture. Hold a damp cloth over the spot until it comes unstuck. Fingers can be unstuck by rolling a pencil gently between them. Eyes can be unstuck by holding a damp cotton-wool pad over the eye.

Epoxy adhesives These consist of a glue and a hardener mixed together just before use. They can be removed with methylated spirit before they set. Once hardened, it's impossible to remove them.

Polyvinyl acetate (PVA and filled PVA) Clean off with methylated spirits.

Synthetic rubber adhesives (contact adhesives) Use non-oily nail polish remover or acetone except on acetate fabrics in which case use pure amyl acetate. Then flush with a dry-cleaning solvent.

Rubber-based adhesives Try an oil paint thinner or write to the manufacturer who may have a proprietary product. Don't use paint strippers which are too savage.

Sticky labels and sticky tape Soak, or keep covered with a wet cloth. Rub with methylated or white spirit.

Alcohol

See specific stain e.g. Wine, Beer, Perfume.

Alkalis (such as washing soda, baking soda)

May permanently damage a fabric, particularly polyester or polyester mixtures so wash immediately as for acid. Rinse in cold water and neutralise any last traces with white vinegar. Rinse again.

Anti-perspirants

Treat with dry-cleaning solvent, then household ammonia. Rinse thoroughly.

Ball-point pen

Most ball-point ink is soluble in methylated spirit. Flush repeatedly; the stain may be stubborn. Air or rinse the garment thoroughly.
* On suede try rubbing with an abrasive paper, but only gently, and stop if it looks as though the suede will suffer.

Beer

Treat with white vinegar and rinse. Treat with liquid detergent and rinse. If stain persists, treat with hydrogen peroxide (test fabric first) and rinse. If the fabric is washable, wash at high temperature and dry it in the sun to bleach it.

Bird droppings

Soak washable articles in warm detergent solution following the directions on the packet. Treat non-washables with 60ml household ammonia to 2 litres of water (4 tablespoons to 3½ pints) then with white vinegar and rinse. Or rub with a proprietary pre-wash product.

- On canvas covers and awnings, brush with a stiff brush that has been run across a bar of yellow soap and sprinkled with washing soda crystals. Hose well and rinse.

Blood

Soak or flush out the stain with cold salt water, while still wet if possible. Don't use warm water. If wool, don't rub it, just let the water run through the fabric. If the stain has hardened, brush off as much as possible and soak in a warm solution of liquid detergent following instructions on the packet, or bleach with a hydrogen peroxide solution. Then wash or clean according to fabric.

Butter

Scrape off excess. Wash at high temperature if the fabric is suitable. If not treat with solvent then dry with a hair dryer or wash according to fabric.

Candle wax

Prise off as much as you can. This is easier if you freeze the article for an hour or so then crack the pieces off. Any residue can be sandwiched between sheets of clean brown paper, blotting paper or tissues and ironed with a warm iron. Last remnants of wax should be dissolved and flushed away with a dry-cleaning solvent. Any colour left from the wax should be treated with white spirit and rinsed.

Car polish and wax

Treat with a dry-cleaning solvent, then liquid detergent. Rinse.

Caramel

Flush with cold water, treat with liquid detergent and rinse. If necessary treat with hydrogen peroxide diluted with an equal quantity of water and rinse.

Carbon paper

Treat with undiluted liquid detergent and rinse well. If some stain persists treat with a few drops of household ammonia and then with detergent again. Repeat several times if necessary. On non-washable fabrics, dab with white spirit.

Chewing gum

Freeze for an hour or so and then crack off in small pieces. If you can't get the garment into the freezer, hold ice cubes against the gum. Alternatively soften with egg white before laundering or sponge with a dry-cleaning solvent.
- If the gum has caught in someone's hair, rub ordinary cold cream into the gummed up hair then pull down on the hair strands with an old dry towel so the gum slides off on to the towel.

Chocolate and cocoa

Scrape off residue with a blunt knife. Flush with cold water. Treat with liquid detergent. Rinse. If a slight stain remains, use a dry-cleaning solvent.

Coca-Cola and Pepsi-Cola

Flush with cold water. Treat from the back with a liquid detergent. Rinse. For residual stains, treat with white spirit containing a drop or two of white vinegar then rinse.

Cod-liver oil

Fresh stains are easily removed. Spoon up as much as possible. Sponge on solvent from the back of the stain. Rinse. Old cod-liver oil stains are practically impossible to remove, even with bleach.
- On carpets use a dry-foam carpet shampoo.
- On baby clothes, sponge with a strong solution of mild detergent and wash as usual.

Coffee and tea

Flush immediately and thoroughly with cold water, rinse in cold water. If necessary soak in hand-hot liquid detergent solution then rinse thoroughly. Any remaining stain can be treated when dry with half-and-half hydrogen peroxide and water solution.
- Milky coffee stains should be soaked in detergent solution and washed according to fabric.
- Coffee spilt on carpets should be squirted immediately with a soda water siphon, then given a carpet shampoo (see page 84).

Cosmetics

Treat with dry-cleaning solvent, then a weak household detergent solution with a few drops of ammonia added. See also Rouge.

Cough medicine

Usually in a base of sugar syrup so wash out with detergent and water or flush through from the wrong side. Any residual colouring should be treated with diluted household ammonia then white spirit or amyl acetate.

Crayon

Dab with solvent and flush any residual colour with white spirit. More than this will damage the fabric.

Cream

Rinse in cold water, treat with liquid detergent. Rinse.
- On carpets blot up excess or scrape it off. Use a little dry-cleaning solvent and then a dry-foam carpet shampoo.

Crude oil and creosote

Soften with white spirit so that you can scrape away as much solid matter as possible. Then flush with a dry-cleaning solvent. Seaside shops often sell a proprietary solvent for removing crude oil.

Curry

Soak in diluted household ammonia or white spirit. Bleach if the fabric will take it.

Dripping

Treat as for Butter.

Dyes

Wipe up any splashed or spilt dye immediately with tissues. Rinse immediately with cold water. Don't use hot water, which 'fixes' many dyes. Then treat with liquid detergent and rinse. Treat again with a household ammonia solution and rinse again. Then treat with white spirit or amyl acetate.
- Non-washable items should be professionally dry-cleaned as soon as possible.
- Remember that removing unwanted dye may also remove colours already on the garment so don't expect the impossible.

Egg

Flush with cold water. Treat with liquid detergent following the instructions on the packet. Rinse. Allow to dry and if necessary treat with a dry-cleaning solvent. Soak stubborn stains on white garments in diluted hydrogen peroxide (1 part to 6 parts water) to which 5 drops of ammonia have been added. Rinse well.

Engine oil

Treat with liquid detergent then flush with a dry-cleaning solvent. Repeat the process several times if necessary.

Faeces

Scrape off any solid matter and absorb as much of the rest as you can. Soak in a borax solution for half an hour. Wash as normal. Biological detergent is often recommended, but it is greener and just as effective to use liquid detergent.

Fat, cold

Treat as for Butter.

Fat, hot

On cottons, linens and wool treat with liquid detergent and rinse. Repeat if necessary. Finish off with a dry-cleaning solvent.

- If synthetic clothing gets splashed with hot fat the fibres will be damaged. Do not use dry-cleaning solvent in this case as it may remove the colour and leave white spots. Take it to a professional cleaner instead.

Felt-tip pen

Lubricate the stain with household soap or glycerine and wash as usual. Sponge any residual stain with white spirit.

Fruit and fruit juices

Flush with cold water, then treat with liquid detergent. Rinse. Treat residual stains with a household ammonia solution followed by diluted hydrogen peroxide (1 part to 6 parts water). Rinse again. Wash white cotton or linen at high temperature.

Furniture polish

Treat with dry-cleaning solvent.

Glue

See Adhesives.

Grass and other leafy stains

Treat with white spirit. Dry the fabric then treat with liquid detergent and rinse. On washable fabrics rub the stain with a proprietary pre-wash product or soak in liquid detergent solution before washing.

Gravy

Wipe off excess then flush, sponge, spray with or soak in cold water or cold water and detergent. Treat any residual stain with dry-cleaning solvent.
• On carpets use a carpet shampoo.

Grease

Scrape off as much as possible. Treat with a dry-cleaning solvent then dry with a hair dryer or in the fresh air.
• For white cotton or linen, put a few washing soda crystals in a bowl of hot water and soak the article. This will emulsify the grease.
• Wash delicate fabrics in a solution of borax and water. Make sure the borax is thoroughly dissolved before putting the clothes in.
• Absorb grease from non-washable items (such as felt hats) with Fuller's earth, bran or French chalk. Mix it to a stiff paste with water, put it on the stain and brush it out gently when dry.
• Or place a piece of blotting paper or tissue above and below the fabric and press with a cool iron. The paper will absorb the grease.

Hair dye

Flush out immediately with cold water, then wash in liquid detergent solution. Put a few drops of household ammonia in the rinsing water. Treat residual stains with white spirit and then, if necessary, a hydrogen peroxide solution. Rinse thoroughly.

Ice-cream

Scrape off excess with a spoon or a blunt knife. Soak in warm detergent solution. Treat any residual greasy stain with dry-cleaning solvent.

Ink

This must be caught at once or the stain will be indelible. As a general rule, flush with cold water immediately, then treat with liquid detergent from the back of the stain. Rinse. Repeat until no more colour comes out. Treat remaining stain with lemon juice, then with diluted household ammonia. Rinse thoroughly.
• Dried ink needs an acid to get rid of the stain. Salts of lemon (potassium quadroxalate) or oxalic acid are most effective. Both are deadly poisonous so keep them well labelled and out of reach of

children. Pour boiling water through the stain, then apply the salts as dry powder and spread them around with a matchstick. Pour boiling water through again. Rinse the fabric quickly and thoroughly to prevent the acid rotting it. If the fabric is coloured, dissolve the acid in water and dip the fabric in the solution and then into cold water so it won't affect the colour. Or use a chlorine bleach solution. Test the fabric first.

Ball-point ink See under Ball-point pen.

Coloured writing ink Usually soluble in water. Treat with liquid detergent and rinse two or three times, then treat with liquid detergent solution with a few drops of household ammonia added, and rinse again. If necessary treat with hydrogen peroxide solution and rinse again.

Duplicating ink Flush with white spirit. Treat any residual stain with liquid detergent and rinse. Repeat if necessary.

Duplicating powder DO NOT GET IT WET. If dry, it will brush out completely with a soft brush.

Felt-tip ink See under Felt-tip pen.

Indelible pencil You'll be lucky if you can get this out. Flush two or three times with dry-cleaning solvent then with white spirit. Treat any residual stain with liquid detergent containing a little household ammonia. Rinse thoroughly. As a last resort try hydrogen peroxide solution and a final rinse.

Indian ink Treat with dry-cleaning solvent, then white spirit followed by liquid detergent solution. Rinse.

Marking ink Impossible to remove once dried. Treat with dry-cleaning solvent and repeat several times.

Printing ink Flush with white spirit. Treat residual stain with liquid detergent and rinse.

Typewriter ribbon Flush two or three times with a dry-cleaning solvent then with white spirit. Then treat with a little liquid detergent containing a few drops of ammonia and rinse well. If there's still the trace of a stain, bleach with a hydrogen peroxide solution and rinse again.

Iodine

Moisten with water and place in the sun or on a warm radiator or in the steam from a kettle.
- For non-washable fabrics, flush with white spirit and rinse. If the stain is on acetate fabric, dilute the spirit with 2 parts water.

Iron mould

Cover the stain with salt. Squeeze lemon juice over the salt and leave for an hour. Rinse well. Repeat several times if necessary. Proprietary rust removers may be used on white fabrics.

- Or soak in hydrogen peroxide with a little water.
- Iron mould is very difficult to remove from woollens and silks. Get specialist treatment from a professional launderer or dry-cleaner.

Jams and conserves

Flush with cold water. Treat with liquid detergent. Rinse. If necessary treat with white spirit. Rinse. If necessary, soak in liquid detergent solution. Rinse.

Lacquer

Treat with amyl acetate as often as necessary to remove the stain. Flush with dry-cleaning solvent.

Leather

Leather dyes often contain tannin and, if they have rubbed off on to other materials, are difficult to remove. Apply neat liquid detergent to the stain. Rub in well. Repeat and rinse well. Bleach final traces of colour with hydrogen peroxide solution.

- If the garment is wool or an unwashable fabric, don't rub it but flush the detergent through.

Lipstick

See Cosmetics.

Mascara

See Cosmetics.

Meat juices

Flush with cold water. Soak in liquid detergent. Rinse. Allow to dry and treat residual stains with dry-cleaning solvent.

Metal polish

Flush with water. Treat with liquid detergent and rinse. If necessary, treat with white spirit and rinse again.

Mildew or mould

Wipe books and papers with a clean, soft cloth. Stains can sometimes be bleached out with an ink eradicator. Colours will be bleached out too, of course.

- For fabrics flush with diluted bleach from the wrong side. Rinse. Launder as usual.
- For leather, wipe over with undiluted antiseptic mouthwash. Wipe and rub dry with a soft cloth. Polish.
- For shower curtains rub with a mixture of lemon juice and salt or white vinegar and salt.

To prevent mildew Prevention really is better than cure so take the following steps to keep mildew at bay.
- Dry clothes promptly after washing.
- Place chemical moisture absorbers (from chemists) in damp cupboards. Or make your own by tying several pieces of chalk together and hanging them in the cupboard to absorb moisture.
- Use moisture-repellent sprays on shower curtains etc.

Milk

Treat as for Cream.

Mineral oil

Treat with dry-cleaning solvent. Rinse. Saturate fabric with water, pour or dab on lemon juice while wet and rinse again.

Modelling materials (eg Plasticine, Playdough)

Pick off as much as possible with fingernails or blunt knife. Use liquid detergent solution or dry-cleaning solvent to remove remnants.

Mud

Allow to dry. Brush off. Any residual stain can be treated with dry-cleaning solvent, then with white spirit followed by liquid detergent, and finally rinsed.

Mustard

Flush with cold water. Treat with liquid detergent. Rinse.

Nail varnish

Treat with amyl acetate.
- You can use non-oily nail varnish remover or acetone, but not on acetate fabrics.

Ointment

Dab with dry-cleaning solvent. Rinse in cold water. Treat with liquid detergent. Rinse.

Paints and lacquers

Acrylic paint Absorb with tissues. Wash out with detergent solution. Use a dry-cleaning solvent or white spirit to remove residue. Test synthetics first.

Cellulose paints (eg model aircraft paints) Treat with cellulose thinners. Do not use on viscose.

Emulsion paint Will wash out easily in cold water while still wet. Once dry it's impossible to remove.

Enamel paint Treat with white spirit or a proprietary paint remover while still wet.

Oil paint Sponge wet paint with white spirit or dry-cleaning solvent then rinse. Dried oil paint may be removed with a proprietary paint remover. Rinse thoroughly afterwards.

Perfume

Treat with household ammonia straight from the bottle. Rinse thoroughly. Or soak in detergent solution then wash as usual.

- Residual stains can be removed with hydrogen peroxide solution on wet fabric. Rinse.

Perspiration

Wet the fabric and treat with household ammonia straight from the bottle. Rinse thoroughly. Or try soaking in a detergent solution. If the stain persists, wet the fabric again and treat with hydrogen peroxide solution and rinse.

- If anti-perspirant deodorant is combined with the stain, treat with a dry-cleaning solvent, then use household ammonia as described above.
- If dye is combined with the stain, try treating it with white vinegar.
- Treat white linen and cotton by soaking the stain in an eggcupful of white spirit to which 5 drops of household ammonia have been added.
- For silk and wool use diluted hydrogen peroxide. Sponge the stain or soak for 5 to 15 minutes then rinse thoroughly and wash as usual.
- For viscose, nylon and polyesters, use dilute liquid bleach solution. Don't soak viscose garments for long, as they become weak while wet.

Resin

Treat with dry-cleaning solvent or white spirit from the wrong side. Test for colour fastness (see page 38). Rinse in cold water. On acetate fabric, dilute the spirit with 2 parts water before using.

Rouge

Treat with dry-cleaning solvent. Repeat two or three times. Rinse and dry then treat with liquid detergent solution followed by household ammonia solution. Rinse.

Rust

(See also Iron mould.) Treat with lemon juice and rinse. Proprietary rust removers can be used on white fabrics.

Sauce

Flush with cold water, treat with liquid detergent solution for the grease. When dry, treat with white spirit. Rinse.

Scorch marks

Damp the scorched area with 1 part glycerine to 2 parts water, rubbing in the solution with the finger tips. Then soak in a solution of 50g borax to 600ml warm water (1 tablespoon to 1 pint). Leave it for 15 minutes. Rinse well.

- A traditional cure is to polish the mark with the edge of a bevelled coin.

Shiny patches

Dark fabrics show up shine more than light ones.
- Some dry-cleaners offer a de-shining service.
- Very gently rub the shiny parts with very fine-grade glass-paper.
- A traditional cure for shine is to simmer ivy leaves in water until tender and use the liquid for sponging the shiny patches, after brushing the garment.
- A traditional colour restorer for black clothes is to brush them all over with distilled water containing a few drops of liquid ammonia.

Shoe polish

Treat with a dry-cleaning solvent, then a liquid detergent solution with a few drops of household ammonia added. Rinse. Residual stains may be removed with white spirit.

Soft drinks

Treat as for Fruit and fruit juices.

Soot

Sprinkle with salt, wait half an hour, then vacuum.

Spirits

Flush with cold water, treat with methylated spirit. Rinse. Treat residual stains with hydrogen peroxide solution. Rinse.

Stove polish (eg Zebrite)

Absorb as much as possible by sprinkling with salt and brushing with a soft brush until most of the stain has gone. Treat with dry-cleaning solvent from the wrong side.

Tar, bitumen or pitch

Rub with grease such as margarine, lard or peanut butter, then launder out both tar and grease.
• Or see Crude oil and creosote.

Tarnish

Flush with white vinegar or lemon juice. Rinse well. If the acid in the tarnish changes the colour of a dye, sponge with diluted household ammonia or a solution of bicarbonate of soda and water.

Tea

See Coffee.

Tobacco

Flush with cold water. Treat with white vinegar and rinse. If necessary, treat with liquid detergent containing a little methylated spirit. Or treat with dilute hydrogen peroxide. Rinse.

Toothpaste and dentifrice

Flush out with water.

Treacle

Flush with cold water. Soak in liquid detergent solution. Launder as usual.

Turmeric

See Curry.

Typewriter ribbon

See Ink.

Unidentified stains

If the garment is washable, rinse it in cold water and then wash as usual.
• Non-washable or delicate garments should be taken to a professional dry-cleaner.

Urine

Flush with cold water immediately. Treat with household ammonia straight from the bottle. Then treat with white vinegar or lemon juice and warm detergent solution. If necessary treat with diluted hydrogen peroxide.
• On carpets blot between applications with a clean terry towel or kitchen tissues.

Vaseline

See Grease.

Vegetable oil (cooking oil, castor oil, linseed oil etc)

Treat with dry-cleaning solvent, several times if necessary. Saturate the fabric with water and treat with white spirit with a little vinegar added. Rinse.

Walnut

Stains caused by the outsides of walnuts are virtually impossible to remove. Very fresh stains on white cottons and linens may be boiled in detergent solution. Old stains will leave a grey colour which may respond to a strong chlorine or hydrogen peroxide bleach solution.

• Non-washable fabrics cannot be treated at home. The only hope is a professional dry-cleaner.

Watercolour paint

Flush with cold water. Residual stains can be treated with household ammonia straight from the bottle used on wet fabric. Rinse very thoroughly.

• Or wet the fabric and treat with hydrogen peroxide diluted half and half with water. Rinse.

Wax polish

Treat with dry-cleaning solvent then with liquid detergent. Rinse.

Wine

Treat with liquid detergent. Rinse. Apply white vinegar. Rinse. Remove any slight residual stain with hydrogen peroxide diluted half and half with water.

Xerox powder

Brush out powder immediately. As long as it doesn't get wet it should all come out. Don't use solvent.

Zinc and castor oil ointment

Dampen the stained area. Apply white spirit. Leave for a few minutes. Rinse in warm water.

5
Dry-cleaning

Certain fabrics are unsuitable for washing and should be dry-cleaned. This is because some garments may be made mainly of one fabric but have a lining of another and an interlining of yet another. Or there may be buttons, trimming and zips held together by sewing thread, all of which may be unsuitable for washing.

Sometimes care labels specify a particular type of solvent, so always check before you hand a garment over to the cleaner and point this out to them.

Even if the care label does not say so, many washable garments can be dry-cleaned and sometimes dry-cleaning is actually more satisfactory. But if the label says dry-clean only, don't attempt to wash the garment.

If you have any doubt about the fabric or what the stain is or the right procedure to follow, or if the garment is a valuable one, don't risk damaging it. Get clothes to the cleaner as soon as you can. If they are just grubby you don't want them to absorb the dirt, and if they are stained then the sooner you deal with the stain the more likely it will be to come out completely.

Tell the cleaner what the fabric is made of and what was spilled on it. He will have a variety of chemicals to treat specific stains and, just as important, the correct techniques for removing them. Attempting such work yourself may 'fix' the stain after which even a professional cleaner won't be able to get rid of it. As one professional said to me: 'If in doubt, don't fiddle with it. I'm always getting people who say "I have spilled egg on this sheepskin coat. I haven't touched it at all – just held it over the kettle for a bit"; so they've shrunk the leather and cooked the egg. If they'd brought it straight to me they would have got the coat back clean and wearable.'

How often should clothes be cleaned?

People are curiously inconsistent. They will wash most of their clothes every few days, but wouldn't dream of having a suit cleaned more than once or twice a year, whereas suits should be cleaned about once a month or every 15 wearings or so. Silk shirts should be cleaned much more often and so should raincoats which must be automatically reproofed by the cleaner or they will become permanently discoloured.

How dry-cleaning works

Dry-cleaning is not really dry. All dry-cleaning machines use a solvent of some kind which dissolves grease, oil and wax. In fact a dry-cleaning machine does exactly the same things as a washing-machine but uses a dry-cleaning fluid instead of water. Dry-cleaning should also remove water-soluble stains such as sweat, and stains of food and drink, cooking splashes, mud, blood, oil and graphite (from trapping a coat in the car door, for instance).

The solvents

There are four main types of dry-cleaning solvents used by professionals. These are trichloroethane, perchloroethylene, fluorocarbon and white spirit. (Carbon tetrachloride, which used to be common, has been found to be extremely toxic, is not used in commercial machines and should never be used or even kept in the house.)

The most commonly used solvent is perchloroethylene which is entirely satisfactory for many garments, household furnishings and fabrics.

The other commonly used solvent is fluorocarbon, which is less powerful and won't start to dissolve buttons or finishes, bindings or interlinings. It has a low boiling point so can be reclaimed after use by distillation. Fluorocarbon is the best solvent to use for acrylics and other heat-sensitive fabrics and for suede and leather. It boils at less than the temperature of a cup of hot tea. Unfortunately fluorocarbon is distinctly not 'green' and will probably be phased out over the next ten years.

Grease-based stains generally will not come out with solvent alone. A small amount of water in the right form is also needed. With wool, however, water must not be used and it is very important to make sure the cleaner is aware that a garment is made of wool.

The solvent dissolves oils, waxes and grease and releases particles of dirt. After 4 to 7 minutes the solvent is drained from the drum and the garment is spun, then rinsed in clean solvent and given another high speed spin. Warm air is blown into the drum to dry the garments while they tumble. With perchloroethylene the drying temperature is around 60°C (140°F) but with fluorocarbon it need only reach 30°C (86°F). Detergent is often added during the first part of the process to disperse the water evenly (if water is used at all) and to suspend the dust particles and prevent them from going back into the fabric.

All solvents used in dry-cleaning at present are non-flammable but they are also anaesthetics. Small amounts will give you a headache, make you giddy, and possibly even make you unconscious.

Dry-cleaning in a launderette

The coin-operated dry-cleaning machines found in launderettes are not as effective as the more sophisticated machines used by professional dry-cleaners: the solvent is not always distilled, many just filter out a fair amount of the dirt, there may be no rinsing programme and they may not remove all spots and stains. What's more you will usually have to do the pressing at home.

Coin-ops are useful as budget cleaning for curtains, coats and blankets but delicate fabrics or valuable items should not be cleaned in them.

Some hints on using coin-operated machines

- A usual load for a coin-operated machine is about 4.5 to 5.5kg (10 to 12lb). Don't overload a dry-cleaning machine.
- Make sure the clothes are completely dry before you take them out of the machine. If you put in more clothes than the machine is supposed to take they will come out not quite dry and the residual vapour, which is toxic, may make you giddy or even unconscious. If the machine stops before it is supposed to, call the manager, don't try to deal with it yourself.
- Don't put soft toys in a dry-cleaning machine as they will take much longer to dry out and the fumes could be deadly to a child hugging a teddy in bed.
- Always read all the instructions carefully before using a dry-cleaning machine.

DEALING WITH PROFESSIONAL DRY-CLEANERS

There is no easy way to find a good cleaner. The introduction of fully automated machines using non-flammable cleaning fluid has made it possible to install machines in high street shops, so there are usually plenty to choose from. Find one who will give a personal service where you can get advice direct from the man with the machine and where there may be a mending and button-sewing-on service on the premises.

Some cleaners invite you to pay extra for a more careful finish. For special clothes this is worthwhile.

If you want a specialist cleaner for a particular item such as a duvet or particularly delicate silk, look in the Yellow Pages for local specialists or ask the Textile Services Association (see Addresses).

Cleaners can offer a variety of services. Much of the work has to be done by hand which is why it's quite expensive. 'Spotting' is the removal of specific stains from a fabric. It has to be done by skilled personnel with a knowledge of fabrics, chemicals and what has caused the stain. Some stains come out in the normal cleaning process – any that still show are treated before pressing so they will not be set in. Old stains may be impossible to get rid of. A good cleaner will tell you when this is so.

Steam pressing and shaping also have to be done by hand using a variety of different presses, steam finishes and specialised small appliances (such as 'steam puffs' for shaped garments) and hand irons. Pleats are set by hand, linings and underskirts and all elaborate clothes are ironed by hand. Cleaning personnel usually specialise in suit pressing, pleating or silk finishing, for instance.

Most cleaners display a list of prices covering items most often brought in to be cleaned. Prices for other standard articles or services will be quoted on request. Where articles are of exceptional value or of an unusual nature, cleaners may charge a special price.

Special services

- Many dry-cleaners will do small repairs and alterations. Replacing buttons may be included in the overall cleaning charge or there may be a small extra charge.
- Many cleaners will put new zips in. Some are better at it than others and prices vary so it pays to shop around.
- Retexturing is a special service. It impregnates the fabric with a dressing which renews the set and the way it will hang. It gives firmer pleats and is specially helpful for old, tired looking clothes. Many clothes don't need retexturing, however. Don't ask for

knitted materials, woollens or lightweight fabrics to be retextured. The retexturing fluid may be a crease-resistant or crease-retaining resin or a waterproofing agent.

- Dry cleaning itself is one of the best methods of mothproofing but a special treatment can be applied which will give even more protection until the next cleaning.

Things that need special care

Wool

This needs special attention when washing or dry-cleaning. Wool thread has a coating of scales which work against each other when in water, making the garment felt and shrink. This doesn't happen in solvent. The looser the knitting the more the wool is likely to shrink. Once shrunk, wool cannot be unshrunk. Make sure the cleaner knows he is dealing with wool so that he won't put water in with the solvent mixture.

Furnishings

- Curtains, eiderdowns, duvets, pillows, cushions, loose covers etc, can all be efficiently dealt with by a specialist cleaner.
- Carpets and upholstery can be cleaned for you at home but cleaning companies sometimes prefer to clean carpets at their works where they can be treated more thoroughly. They will collect and return the carpet. Most companies will offer a silicone treatment to repel dirt and make future cleaning easier.
- Valuable oriental rugs are best treated by specialists.
- Elaborate pelmets may have to be cleaned by hand and may even have to be unpicked and sewn up again afterwards.
- Some cleaners will flame-proof curtains and upholstery fabrics as well as stage wardrobes etc. This treatment has to be repeated every time the items are cleaned.

Leather and suede

Leather and suede cleaning are highly specialised. Some cleaners deal with all kinds of leather garments including sheepskin, which go through a special cleaning process and are dried by special methods too. Suede and sheepskin are usually finished by spraying with oil to keep the skin supple. Dye may be added to the spray to revive faded colours. Many dry-cleaners subcontract the cleaning of suede and leather to specialists.

- Get suede and sheepskin cleaned as soon as dirt begins to show round collar and cuffs. If a garment is allowed to get very dirty the chances of a cleaner getting it really clean again are small.

- Suede and leathers should be cleaned only in perchloroethylene or fluorocarbon.
- For an extra charge most cleaners will repair damaged cuffs, collars and pockets. Some will also touch up colours damaged during wear and many will match up buttons too.
- Advise your cleaner if the garment is being cleaned for the first time. Cleaning can highlight the different skins used and a cleaner can retint by spray.
- After cleaning store under a clean cotton cloth, never plastic, as leather and suede need to breathe.

Velvets

Although velvets are washable, they dry-clean quite satisfactorily and because they are so heavy to handle when wet, this is probably the best method of cleaning.

WHAT TO DO IF THINGS GO WRONG

Although most cleaners will do a perfectly satisfactory job it is useful to know how you stand in the law if things go wrong. Put very simply:

- At common law, if a launderer or cleaner loses or destroys a customer's article through negligence he is liable for the market value of the article at the time it is lost or destroyed. If the article is only damaged and is capable of adequate repair, the launderer/ cleaner is only liable for the cost of that repair.
- The liability of the cleaner is for negligence, that is to say, for breach of a duty or obligation, whether imposed by the common law or by an express or implied term in a contract to take reasonable care or exercise reasonable skill in relation to the articles left with him.
- You can't expect the cleaner to be responsible (unless he adds to the damage by his negligence) for faulty manufacture (colour running or fabric stretching during manufacture, inadequate seaming or incorrect care labelling); previous misuse by the customer (eg drying of razor blades on towels, excessive use of bleach, spillage of acids etc); and normal but unrecognised wear (eg weakening of curtains by exposure to light).

How to complain

If your clothes come back shrunk so as to be unwearable or dyed the wrong colour or irretrievably limp, it may be difficult to find out who is to blame: *the cleaner* who could have used the wrong solvent or dirty solvent or *the manufacturer* who did not label the clothes or made them badly, or *you* because you have previously washed the clothes and not got all the soap out or tried to remove a stain and did some damage in the process.

- If you are absolutely sure it was not your fault, be patient and keep trying.
- Complain as soon as you possibly can. The cleaner may sort things out quickly and simply – they often do. On the other hand it may take ages. Don't give up hope.
- Always keep all relevant papers, letters (including copies of all your letters) and communications. Keep a note of all telephone conversations.
- If the cleaner is a member of the Textile Services Association (which has its own code of practice negotiated with the Office of Fair Trading), he can refer any dispute for concilliation to the association's Customer Advisory Service.
- If the cleaner is not a member of a trade association you can approach your local Citizen's Advice Bureau or Trading Standards Department (look in the Yellow Pages) who may be prepared to negotiate between you and the cleaner.
- Any of these organisations or the cleaner himself may recommend an independent laboratory report. Laboratory testing is expensive and it is advisable to contact several test houses and ask for estimates before proceeding. Whether you or the cleaner send an item for assessment, a copy of the report should be made available to the other party. It is important to give the laboratory notes indicating what you think has happened and a history of how the item has been cleaned before. The cleaner should provide details of cleaning and finishing procedures carried out.
- As a last resort, you can claim for compensation through the County Court. Obtain a booklet outlining procedures from your local County Court or Citizens Advice Bureau.
- If you have been using a coin-operated machine and something goes wrong to damage the clothes, write to or telephone the owner or manager. His address should be pinned up in the premises.

Dry-cleaning – the green way?

Unfortunately the only green way of dry-cleaning is to use solvent-based dry-cleaners as little as possible or not at all. Avoid buying new clothes that have to be dry-cleaned and don't have washable items dry-cleaned – wash them instead.

6
Guidelines
for housework

Hygiene, especially in the kitchen and bathroom is the most important aim but it's not difficult to achieve. This is dealt with in Chapter Seven. As far as the rest of the house goes, it should be kept clean and tidy, but don't become obsessed with spotlessness and tidyness at the cost of spending time with family and friends.

MAKING HOUSEWORK EASIER

The best way of dealing with housework is by creating a home where you don't have to do much! The important thing is to provide a basic order in the home so that cleaning is a simple process, not made impossible by underlying chaos. There are various ways of reducing housework.

A convenient place for everything

A place for everything will make things easier to put away and find, as well as easier to clean. Here are some storage suggestions:
- Bookcases for books – freestanding or built-in shelves.
- Storage near the cooker for pots, pans and casseroles.
- Cup hooks for cups.
- Hanging storage for kitchen implements, telephone, and anything else you can get off tables and work surfaces or out of drawers.
- Boxes, baskets or shelves for different categories of toys.
- Sensible storage for sewing equipment and other hobbies, eg a chest of drawers, a specially designed sewing box or a collection of baskets.
- Filing boxes for family papers and a spike for unpaid bills.

- Hanging storage for anything you can get off the floor: eg iron and ironing board, cleaning equipment, tools, folding chairs.
- Convenient shelves for phone books, cookery books, pen and pencil pots, china, glass etc.
- Keep all cleaning products out of the reach of children and not under the kitchen sink.

Don't gather junk

Don't surround yourself with more possessions or furniture than you need or can find room for.
- Throw out worn clothes, broken toys, old Christmas cards, useless bits of fabric, ugly furniture. If it's too good to throw away take it to the local charity shop.
- Don't buy odd little flea-market bits of junk unless you have a use or a place for them. If you collect things, make a space where they can be displayed and lit.
- Don't collect up electrical gadgets or any other gadgets unless you need them. Anything that has remained unused for six months will probably never be used, so throw or give away.

Stop dirt getting in

If dirt, dust and soot aren't allowed into the home in the first place, then cleaning will be easier.
- Make sure windows and doors are well fitting and don't allow dust to blow in.
- Install a really big door mat or even fitted door matting (available by the metre) which will help to capture much dust and dirt on its way in.
- Suggest that people abandon their shoes at the front (or back) door, especially if you live in the country or have a clayey garden.

Choose efficient housework tools

Good tools will make housework easier and more pleasant to do. Choose tools which are comfortable to handle, good to look at and easy to care for.

Obviously what you need will depend on whether you live in a large house with a family and pets or alone in a small flat. Here's a list of suggestions.
- Vacuum cleaner or carpet sweeper
- Broom
- Floor mop, sponge mop or other 'wet' mop
- Dry mop

- Dustpan and brush (or two brushes – one soft, one hard)
- Cloths: dusters, dishcloths, floor cloths, tea towels, kitchen paper, disposable cloths, chamois or scrim for cleaning windows
- Scourers
- Lavatory brush and holder
- Washing up brushes – useful for cleaning baths, basins and sinks as well as washing up. You should have a separate one for pets' dishes. Use different colours for different uses.

Care of equipment

Properly cared for equipment means efficient and economical equipment with a longer life so it's worth spending time maintaining it properly.

- It's important to keep all cleaning equipment clean and dry when not in use. This is particularly true of cloths. Dishcloths are the most likely cloths to harbour germs, since they are in contact with old food on plates and may remain moist for some time. Bacteria flourish in the warm and damp atmosphere of kitchens and bathrooms but they will not survive on cloths if they are allowed to dry out. So it is important to rinse out cloths (including dishcloths, floor cloths, face cloths and bath sponges) every time they are used and hang them to dry as quickly as possible. It is more hygienic to use disposable cloths and throw them away frequently than to hang on to fabric cloths which are never quite clean or dry.
- Wash dustpan and brush in warm detergent solution and leave in a warm place to dry, preferably outside. Do this once a month or when it begins to look grubby.
- Wash broom in warm detergent solution once a month or so. If you wish to use it as a cobweb brush, wash it and dry it thoroughly before you do so.
- Change the sponge in a floor mop before it becomes so worn that it scratches the flooring.
- Change the vacuum bag frequently. A full bag is inefficient and makes the motor work too hard. Wipe the outside of the vacuum cleaner with a cloth wrung out in detergent solution.
- Empty carpet sweepers after each use. The little boxes don't hold much but they do pick up a lot.
- Regularly check flexes and plugs on electrical equipment for wear. Replace if necessary.
- Rinse mop heads thoroughly and dry completely before putting away.
- Hang brooms, mops and anything else which will hang, on a wall rather than allow them to stand on their bristles.

- New bristle brooms last longer if dipped in cold salted water before use. But don't do this to nylon or plastic bristles.
- Clean the broom cupboard occasionally: take everything off the walls and shelves and brush down with the broom before cleaning the walls with a solution of mild disinfectant or vinegar. Leave the door open while you allow the surfaces to dry.

How often should you clean what?

There are no hard and fast rules about this. Here are some guidelines.

Daily

- Wash pet dishes and clean out cat litter tray.
- Empty ash trays.
- Make beds and put clothes away.
- Clean lavatory, basin and kitchen sink.
- Put rubbish in plastic bags, tie tops and put in dustbin.
- Rinse out cloths and hang in a warm, dry place.
- Clean up any spills and sweep or vacuum if and when necessary.

Weekly (or as necessary)

- Vacuum living areas (some people do this daily).
- Wipe out refrigerator and throw away old food.
- Do the laundry.
- Shake out pets' bedding and clean bird cages.
- Sweep front steps and back yard.
- Change bed linen.

Monthly

- Clean windows and mirrors.
- Polish silver and metalware.
- Thoroughly clean the cooker.
- Clean dustbin.
- Clean filters in washing machine.
- Clean central heating radiators (winter).
- Give one room in the house a thorough clean.

Twice a year

- Defrost fridge (even if it's an automatically defrosting one).
- Descale coffee machine, kettle and steam iron, if you live in a hard water area.
- Clean out gutters and downpipes.
- Polish wooden furniture.

- Clean out cupboards and take worthwhile unwanted things to a charity shop.

Once a year

- Spring clean the entire home.

CLEANING A ROOM – THE RIGHT WAY

Rooms in general

1 Open windows.
2 Empty vases of dead flowers, empty ash trays and waste paper baskets, throw away old newspapers.
3 Put away toys, magazines, books, games, correspondence etc.
4 Clean out grates and re-lay fires if you have open fires or solid fuel stoves.
5 Move furniture – out of the room if possible, or at least so you can get behind it.
6 Vacuum curtains, upholstery and carpets.
7 Mop and polish surrounds.
8 Clean windows.
9 Wipe or dust window ledges, wainscotting, polished furniture. Polish where necessary.
10 Shake rugs outside before replacing them.
11 Dust pictures and objects, desks, tables, chairs, shelves etc.

Bedrooms

1 Put items for washing in laundry basket.
2 Line up boots and shoes to be cleaned.
3 Strip and air the bed.
4 Dust, brush and vacuum the bedstead and mattress. Turn the mattress. Make the bed.
5 Remove all ornaments and cosmetics from the dressing table, lay them on a cloth on the bed.
6 Dust and polish dressing table.
7 Shake curtains.

Kitchen and bathrooms

Chapter 7 deals exclusively with cleaning these two important rooms.

Cleaning a room – the lazy way

- Generally tidy the room.
- Vacuum and sweep only where it noticeably needs it. Otherwise pick up odd bits of fluff and sewing cotton with your fingers and leave it at that.
- Dust and wipe surfaces only where they noticeably need it.
- Clean windows only when the glass begins to look smudgy in sunlight.
- Vacuum bedstead and turn the mattress only once every two months.
- It is tempting but not recommended to sweep dust under a rug or piece of furniture – it only leads to more work later on, so isn't really time-saving in the end.

Cleaning a room – the green way

- Use the minimum amount of detergents and chemicals.
- Don't use aerosol spray polishes.
- Don't use aerosol air-fresheners: rather make your own pot pourri or hang bunches of dried herbs around the room, keep windows open and upholstery and carpets clean, and don't smoke in the house.
- Use fly papers rather than aerosol or long-term release insecticides.
- Use natural products such as white vinegar, lemon juice, and bicarbonate of soda instead of toxic and polluting proprietary household cleaners, many of which don't even list their ingredients on the packaging.
- Use detergents with as few additives as possible: no phosphates, perfumes or enzymes please.

SPRING CLEANING

Theoretically spring cleaning is a thing of the past, but there's a lot to be said for a good, thorough clear-out once a year and spring is the best time to do it, when the first sunbeams show up grimy windows and flecks of dust.

This is also a good time to check for repairs and any exterior work which needs doing, such as gutter clearing or the odd roof tile being replaced.

Internal spring cleaning checklist

1 Give each room a thorough going-over as described on pages 64–5, remembering the normally untouched areas such as behind doors, above door frames, under tables and chests of drawers etc.
2 Turn out cupboards and ruthlessly throw away 'useful' objects you have not used for the past year.
3 Get chimneys swept if you have open fires.
4 Take out books and dust them and the shelves.
5 Get gas appliances serviced.
6 Sort out and dispose of clothes you never use.
7 Clean upholstery and curtains.
8 Clean carpets and rugs or get them professionally cleaned.
9 Clear out the linen cupboard. Throw away worn sheets and duvet covers or turn them sides to middle or cut them up to make dusters.
10 Wash duvet covers or have them cleaned.
11 Get electric blankets serviced. This is necessary for safety as well as hygiene.
12 Clean windows downstairs (see page 93). Get a window cleaner to do the upstairs windows.
13 Wash walls and paintwork if you haven't been wiping them clean throughout the year. The paintwork in homes where people smoke nearly always needs a thorough wash.
14 Clear out larder, kitchen cupboards and drawers. Throw away any pieces of cracked and broken china as they may harbour germs.
15 Defrost and clean out the freezer (see page 69).
16 Clean or replace the filter on cooker hood and extractor fan.
17 Oil metal curtain rails and sliding door tracks.
18 Remove and clean light fittings.

External spring cleaning checklist

1 Clear out gutters, downpipes and rainwater gulleys.
2 Check windows for joints and crevices where water might lodge. Clean down exterior window frames and use a rust primer for rusty patches on metal frames.
3 Check the roof for loose or broken slates or tiles.
4 Check the pointing on outside walls. Damaged pointing allows the walls to absorb water which will eventually damage the material and allow damp into the house.

7
Cleaning the kitchen and bathroom

The kitchen and the bathroom are the rooms that require the most thorough cleaning because each produces potentially more bacteria than any other room in the house, and because they create warm, steamy atmospheres where those bacteria can thrive. Salmonella scares have reminded us all how important it is to keep the kitchen and everything in it spotlessly clean and germ free.

It is important to keep surfaces in both rooms clean and dry at all times, to rinse cloths whenever they are used, to dry them quickly and to wash hands after cleaning or before any food preparation.

Chapters 8 and 9 deal with cleaning floors, walls and ceilings. This chapter concentrates on fixtures and contents specific to kitchens and bathrooms.

KITCHEN

For maximum efficiency and hygiene kitchen appliances should be regularly cleaned. Don't allow the dirt to build up – particularly on ovens and hobs – or the eventual task of cleaning will be far more difficult and unpleasant.

Cooker

Solid fuel cookers

These should be wiped after each use. Follow the instructions in the manufacturer's booklet.

- Hotplates should be rubbed with a wire brush frequently so that the surface is completely flat and free of grit or crumbs. Their efficiency depends on the bottom of the pan meeting the cooking surface at all points.

- Hot ovens on solid fuel cookers are self-cleaning because the heat burns away any deposits.
- The cool oven can be cleaned with a cloth wrung out in detergent solution or water with an eggcupful of vinegar added. Cool ovens don't usually need much cleaning because grease doesn't spit in them.
- Clean vitreous enamel areas with liquid detergent solution.

Gas and electric hobs

Before cleaning an electric oven or hob switch it off at the mains.
- Don't soak any electrical parts in water.
- After using the hob, allow to cool then take off removable parts. Wash in the sink in hot water and detergent. Wipe over the whole cooker and rub stubborn grease spots or burned-on food with a nylon scourer. Don't scrape the surfaces with a knife, even a blunt one.
- Clean really dirty hobs with a proprietary caustic jelly applied with an old toothbrush. Leave it on for an hour or two and rinse it off with warm water. Wear gloves to protect your hands.
- For a green way of cleaning the hob, use white vinegar.

Gas and electric ovens

There are various oven-cleaning products available. Some can be used in a cold oven. They are nearly all caustic. If the oven is very dirty, you may have to rub it with wire wool as well.
- Bicarbonate of soda used on a damp cloth is the green way to clean ovens.
- Self-cleaning ovens or those with detachable non-stick sides should be cleaned according to the manufacturer's instructions. Don't use caustic oven cleaners on them.
- Glass doors can be cleaned with bicarbonate of soda and a gentle rub with wire wool.

Grill

This should burn itself clean. It can be wiped with liquid detergent solution if necessary.

Microwave ovens

- Wipe the interior with a damp cloth after every use.
- Clean the outside with a cream cleaner.
- The green way is to stand a bowl of hot water with a slice of lemon in it in the oven. Bring to the boil and boil until the interior is good and steamy. Then wipe the interior with a damp cloth.

Extractor fans and cooker hoods

Extractor fans

Switch off fan and unplug or turn the electricity off at the mains.
- Remove outer cover and wash in warm water and detergent.
- Wipe fan blades with a damp cloth. Don't get them wet.
- Dry everything and replace cover.

Cooker hood

Clean outside regularly to prevent grease building up.
- Every six months to a year clean or replace the filter or it may catch fire. Some have a light to indicate when the filter needs replacing. The more frying you do the more often the filter will need attention.

Refrigerator

Refer to the instruction manual for the recommended way of cleaning your refrigerator.
- Wipe up anything spilled in the fridge at once.
- Non-automatic fridges should be defrosted once a week or once a fortnight or they will run inefficiently.
- The freezing section (condenser) should only need cleaning once a year.
- Even automatically defrosting fridges must be cleaned manually from time to time.
- When defrosting, lift out all removable trays, drawers and shelves. Wash them and the fridge interior in warm detergent solution or wipe with a cloth dipped in bicarbonate of soda. Don't use anything abrasive.
- Wipe the outside with detergent solution or, for a greener way, with white vinegar and water.
- Switch off the electricity and clean the back of the fridge with the brush attachment of the vacuum cleaner.

- Bags filled with carbon (available from hardware stores) will absorb smells in the fridge. So will an eggcupful of bicarbonate of soda placed inside the fridge. Replace every six months or when smells are no longer absorbed.
- If you go away and turn off the electricity, remove all food, wipe out the fridge and leave the door open or the whole interior will become mouldy.

Freezer

If you keep the door or lid tightly closed, opening and closing it as little as possible, then the freezer should only need defrosting once a year, and that is the time to clean it. Choose a time when stock is low – January and February are usually good months, coming after Christmas but before you've stocked it up with garden produce. In any case, the freezer should be defrosted when frost has built up to 5mm (¼in).

1 Disconnect the electricity and remove any frozen foods.
2 Wrap food in several layers of old newspaper and put a blanket or duvet round the whole lot.
3 Make sure any drainage holes are unblocked and place a container or tray under them to collect water.
4 To hasten defrosting, place pans or buckets of hot water in the freezing compartment. Don't use any sharp implement to scrape the ice off in an attempt to speed things up.
5 Mop up water and ice. A large old bath towel will save a lot of cloth-wringing.
6 Wipe the interior with a cloth wrung out in a solution of bicarbonate of soda and water. Wipe with a dry cloth.
7 Switch on the electricity and put the food back.
8 Wipe the outside of the cabinet with warm water and detergent.

Sink

- Clean after each use with a proprietary cream cleaner or detergent solution. You may find initial cleaning easier with an angled washing up brush rather than a cloth. Wipe dry.
- Keep the sink overflow and plughole clear by using a small toothbrush or bottle brush kept for the purpose.
- Occasionally place a handful of washing soda crystals over the outlet and pour a kettle of hot water over them to keep the S-bend clean and clear.
- From time to time rub the taps with half a cut lemon and leave for a few minutes then wipe dry. This gets rid of limescale.

Worktops

Remove everything from the worktop before you begin cleaning it. Food preparation areas should be wiped after every use to prevent the transfer of bacteria from contaminated food (eg raw meat) to uncontaminated food.

Laminated tops Wipe with a damp cloth dipped in bicarbonate of soda.

Untreated wooden tops Rub with teak oil or linseed oil.
- Treat heat marks with equal parts of linseed oil and cleaning fluid and wipe off. Or try lemon juice or a proprietary wood bleach.

Slate worktops Wipe with a cloth dipped in milk to give a matt lustre.

Marble worktops Wipe regularly with a cloth wrung out in mild detergent solution. Or wipe it over *quickly* with lemon juice or white vinegar.
- Marble is porous so don't let water or any other liquid sit on it.

Ceramic tops These just need wiping with a damp cloth or lemon juice.

Kitchen cupboards and larders

Clean out food cupboards or larders once a month or so. Crockery and glass cupboards will probably need cleaning out only about once a year.

1 Remove everything from the shelves.
2 Clean inside thoroughly with detergent solution, especially in the corners, making sure you get rid of all crumbs.
3 Leave doors open while surfaces dry.
4 Throw away old opened jars and tins.
5 Wipe all jars and bottles with warm detergent solution. Dry then replace in cupboard or larder.
6 Wash any crockery and glass that hasn't been used for some time. Replace in cupboard.

Cleaning electrical gadgets

Switch off and disconnect all appliances from the mains before cleaning and don't put any electrical parts in water.
- Wipe the exteriors of all kitchen machinery frequently with a damp cloth.
- Chrome can be cleaned with a damp cloth dipped in bicarbonate of soda. Don't use scouring pads or abrasive cleaners.
- Clean all equipment used for preparing food immediately after use.
- Leave the sharp blades and discs of blenders, and food processors on the worktop or soaking in a small bowl until you are ready to

wash them. Clean them one at a time under running water, using a brush.
- Use a toothbrush to get rid of oily deposits in the base of mixers.
- Turn the toaster upside down and shake out the crumbs.
- Treat furred-up kettles with a proprietary descaler, following the manufacturer's instructions. Or cover the element with white vinegar, bring to the boil, allow to cool and pour the vinegar away. Rinse well. Boil up some water and pour that away before using the kettle again.

WASHING UP – THE RIGHT WAY

Washing up is everyone's least favourite chore but if you go about it *the right way* it should be relatively painless. See chapters 12 and 13 for how to clean metal pots, pans and baking trays.

1 First clear the decks: see that the draining board and plate rack are empty and ready for use.
2 Stack up dirty plates and dishes and leave cutlery in a bowl or jug of warm water to make it easier to wash. Keep wood, bone and ivory handles out of the water.
3 Fill the washing-up bowl with hot water and just enough detergent to deal with the grease. The hotter the water, the quicker it will evaporate from items put to drain and the less drying you will have to do.
4 Scrape off uneaten food into the bin and rinse coffee grounds and tea leaves etc.
5 Wash the cleaner items first, eg glasses, and the greasy items last. Wash each piece separately. Lift stemmed glasses by the stem.
6 After washing rinse everything in a bowl of clean warm water or under the tap. Don't use cold water or the sudden change in temperature from hot to cold could cause glasses and china to crack.
7 Put cutlery directly into a cutlery drainer; knives sharp side down. Never leave knives or food processor blades in the washing-up water; someone may put their hand in and cut themselves.
8 Stack items carefully in the draining rack and on the draining board.
9 Dry and polish items with a clean dry tea towel.
10 Put items away as soon as they are dry.
11 Wipe down the sink and draining board.

Washing up – the lazy way

- Soak burned-on food overnight.
- Fit a wall-mounted plate rack above the draining board and store plates in it permanently, putting them there after washing up and without bothering to dry them.
- Allow cutlery and crockery to drain dry without using a tea towel.
- Make those who have not done the cooking do the washing up.
- Use a dishwasher (see below).

Washing up – the green way

- Use a washing-up bowl rather than filling a large sink with water.
- Don't use detergent unless you live in a hard water area, and then very little. In soft water areas hot water alone should be sufficient for washing up with.
- Don't rinse items under a hot running tap as it's very wasteful. Instead use a separate bowl of clean water.
- In summer save the bowl of rinsing water to water the garden with.

Using a dishwasher

- Use the recommended brand of detergent and rinse aid.
- Don't use too much detergent, especially in soft water areas or if your machine has a built in water softener – in which case refill with water softener regularly.
- Load carefully, checking that no items will obstruct the jets of water or the revolving spray arm (if your machine has one). Similarly don't block the detergent dispenser outlet.
- Stack items with their rims facing downwards.
- Don't put silver cutlery in the same basket as stainless steel.
- Anchor lightweight or unstable items between other items.
- Empty the machine as soon as the drying cycle is completed.
- Don't dishwash thin or heat sensitive plastics, wooden bowls, insulated ware, glass with metal trim, delicate china or cut glass, ironware, lacquered metals or high gloss aluminium.
- Avoid running the dishwasher half empty. It's more economical and 'greener' to wait until you have a full load.

BATHROOM

Keep the bathroom as clean and dry as you can at all times. The flushing of the lavatory produces a fine spray of infected water droplets, whether the lid is closed or not. These will land on doors and walls so regular wiping down of all bathroom surfaces with a mild detergent solution is important.

- As well as surfaces, frequently wipe down all bathroom fittings with mild detergent solution.
- Wipe lavatory brush handle and basin, bath and shower tray after each use.
- To clean the lavatory brush hold it under the lavatory flush before allowing it to drain and putting it back in the holder.
- Keep cleaning equipment in obvious and reachable places.

Cleaning baths and sinks – the right way

- Don't use abrasive cleaners or very strong bathroom cleaners on baths, basins or shower trays.
- Clean vitreous enamel baths and ceramic shower trays and basins with cream cleaner applied on a cloth. Rinse well.
- Clean acrylic baths with mild detergent solution. Rub stubborn stains with half a lemon. Rub scratches with silver polish. If necessary use diluted household bleach or hydrogen peroxide but don't leave it on. Rinse well.
- Remove hard water marks with proprietary limescale remover.
- Remove rust marks with proprietary rust remover or use a paste of cream of tartar and hydrogen peroxide and a drop or two of household ammonia. Leave on for an hour or two before wiping clean. Rinse.
- Regularly remove hair balls from plug holes.

Cleaning baths and sinks – the lazy way

- Get everyone to wipe out the bath or sink after they've used it.
- Use a bubble bath that cleans the bath at the same time rather than leaving a tide mark.
- Don't use bath oils.
- Don't allow limescale to build up until it becomes difficult to remove.
- White spirit will usually remove most stubborn greasy stains caused by bath oils etc.

Cleaning baths and sinks – the green way

Instead of proprietary bath cleaning products use vinegar and water or lemon juice.

- Clean hard water marks with vinegar or lemon juice. For stubborn marks soak cotton wool or tissues in white vinegar and leave them on for an hour or so before rubbing the marks away.
- Rub rust stains with a paste made of borax and lemon juice.

Cleaning the lavatory – the right way

- Rub the inside of the toilet bowl every day with the toilet brush and a proprietary cleaner. Remember to clean under the rim. Don't use two different lavatory cleaners at the same time – they may combine to produce explosive or toxic gases.
- Wash seat, handle and surrounds daily. A very dirty lavatory can be emptied of water by pushing the water through with a cloth tied round the lavatory brush. When it is empty, use a proprietary lavatory cleaner in the bowl and leave for an hour or two.

Cleaning the lavatory – the lazy way

Suspend a small block containing detergent, sanitiser and a light perfume under the rim of the bowl. Every time the loo is flushed, some of the cleaner is released. This does NOT eliminate the need to use a lavatory brush entirely or the need to wipe the surrounds daily.

Cleaning the lavatory – the green way

- Use white vinegar instead of proprietary loo cleaners to clean the lavatory and its surrounds.

Cleaning other bathroom items

Shower head

Soak in white vinegar or brush with white vinegar on an old toothbrush.

Bathroom cupboard/medicine chest
- Clear out regularly. Return old medicines to the chemist. It is not safe to flush them down the lavatory or put them in the bin.
- Wipe out the cupboard with a clean cloth.

Bidets
Clean with mild disinfectant or white vinegar and wipe dry. Clean the inside overflow with a toothbrush or bottle brush kept specially for the purpose.

Bath towels and mats
- Wash towels and fabric mats at least once a week and hang them over the side of the bath or over a heated towel rail after use so that they can dry out.
- Wash plastic mats in the sink or basin in warm detergent solution.
- Wipe cork mats with a damp cloth.

Sponges and face flannels
- Rinse thoroughly after use and hang up to dry.
- Wash occasionally in weak vinegar solution (an eggcup of white vinegar to a bowl of water) or in the washing machine. Hang to dry.

Shower curtains
- Remove spots of mildew with bicarbonate of soda on a damp cloth.
- Large areas of mildew should be washed in hot detergent solution and then rubbed with lemon juice. Dry in the sun if possible.
- To machine wash a shower curtain see page 14.

8
Cleaning floors

If you can keep the floor clean, the rest of the house will look basically OK. This is partly because in order to clean the floor properly, you do need to do some clearing and tidying but also because the floor is the background to everything else and whatever it looks like will affect the appearance of the room. So if guests are arriving in 10 minutes and there isn't time to clean everything, get the vacuum and whiz round for an instant transformation.

Sweeping and vacuuming little but often is a good general rule for floors and carpets, but occasionally they do need something more drastic, like washing and polishing or shampooing.

WASHING A FLOOR – THE RIGHT WAY

The following method will remove dirt and old polish, but don't use it for wooden floors which should not get too wet and should just be wiped over with a damp mop. It's best to have two mops for this method and possibly a squeegee – a rubber strip in a holder on the end of a handle, usually used for cleaning windows but excellent for floors too.

1 Move all the furniture out of the room.
   • Slip heavy socks over the legs to make moving easier and to prevent the floor from getting scratched.
2 Sweep or vacuum the floor thoroughly.
3 Apply detergent solution with a sponge or wet mop.
4 Leave detergent for a few minutes so that it can get into the dirt. Don't allow it to run under skirting boards where it may saturate electric wires and sockets.
5 Scrub any very dirty marks and in corners. Use a nylon pad or wire wool if necessary.

6   A squeegee is the ideal tool for scraping up muck from very dirty floors.
7   Afterwards wipe with a nearly-dry mop. Rinse it frequently while working. Rinsing is important so as not to leave a thin film of detergent which will prevent any polish from being absorbed and so make the floor slippery and dangerous.

Washing a floor – the lazy way

Wipe over with a sponge mop squeezed out in a weak detergent solution. Wipe over again with the same mop squeezed out in clear warm water.

Washing a floor – the green way

- Instead of detergent solution use an eggcup of white vinegar in a bowl of water. Very dirty patches can be rubbed with neat vinegar. Leave it on for a few minutes before wiping it clean.
- Many floor-cleaning products contain toxic chemicals such as ethanol, formaldehyde and chlorine, so avoid.

POLISHING FLOORS – THE RIGHT WAY

Don't use too much polish. One application a month or less is quite enough otherwise it will build up into a slippery dirt trap. Just buff up in between from time to time. You can buff up with a piece of waxed paper placed under the mop, which will help to pick up dirt.

There are basically three types of floor polish:

Wax polish

Available as either liquid wax which is easy to apply and helps to clean the floor, or solid wax polish. Both are suitable for unvarnished wood, lino and cork. Solid wax can be thinned with turpentine but why not use liquid wax in the first place?

Liquid solvent polish

The solvent evaporates after application, leaving behind the polish. For wood, lino and cork, as above. Don't use it on thermoplastic or vinyl or anything which the solvent could damage.

Water-based emulsion polish

These types of polish generally have silicones in them. They are easy to apply and long lasting. Use them on any floor except unvarnished or unsealed wood, lino or cork. Be sparing with them because they can build up to become very slippery.

Preparation

Vacuum or sweep up as much grit and dust as you can then remove any big build up of old polish so that you can start again from scratch:

1   Mix a bucket of detergent and water with a little ammonia or, preferably, a bucket of a strong solution of white vinegar and water.
2   Apply with a mop and as soon as dirt and wax begin to dissolve, wipe it all off using a squeegee. Work on a small area at a time and don't let the cleaner sink right in. If you have no squeegee, crumpled newspaper or a sponge mop will do.
3   Wipe off with a clean mop.
4   Move on to the next area.
5   Let the floor dry thoroughly before you apply new polish.

Applying the polish

1   Apply polish evenly and lightly to a clean, dry floor with a soft cloth. Allow to soak in.
2   Buff up with a broom head tied up in an old terry towel or with a 'dumper' (a heavily padded weight on a stick), or use an electric floor polisher (available from hire shops). Or you can, of course, get down on your hands and knees and buff up the floor by hand.
•   Don't apply more polish for another two or three months. Just buff up in between.
•   Build up the surface with two or three thin coats rather than applying one enormously thick one. The first coat should cover the whole floor, the next two only the well worn areas.
•   Don't splash walls etc with polish as it is difficult to remove.
•   To clean floor polisher pads place them between several thicknesses of paper towel and press with a warm iron. The towels will absorb the warm wax.

Polishing floors – the lazy way

1   Don't bother to remove old polish but do make sure the floor is clean and vacuum or sweep up as much grit and dust as you can.
2   Apply polish to a duster tied round the head of a broom. Rub this over the main traffic areas.
3   Buff up with a clean cloth tied round the broom.
•   Or don't apply more polish at all – simply buff up where necessary.

Polishing – the greener way

•   Good polishing practice is to be economical with the polish otherwise the floor may become slippery. This is also the green way.

Less polish means fewer silicones, synthetic solvents and artificial perfumes.
- Do not use aerosol polishes.

SPECIAL TREATMENTS FOR PARTICULAR FLOORS

Certain types of flooring require specialised treatment to maintain their appearance.

Asphalt

Wash occasionally with warm water and mild detergent. Rinse and dry.
- Don't use abrasives or abrasive cleaning powders.
- Don't use old or wax-based polishes. Use a water-based emulsion polish instead.
- Don't apply too much or the floor will become slippery.
- Don't use solvents which will soften the surface.

Ceramic tiles

Mop with mild detergent solution.
- Remove spilled nail varnish by allowing it to dry and then peeling it off.

Concrete

Don't use soap on unsealed concrete floors. Seal the surface to make it easier to sweep and wash. Or use a wax polish.

Cork

Polish plain cork; wash sealed cork. Vinyl-covered cork tiles can be mopped with mild detergent solution.
- Don't allow cork to get very wet and dry it thoroughly after washing.

Floor paint

Paints are available which can be applied to vinyl, lino, wood etc. Painted floors are easier to clean if they have a wax polish or have been varnished or sealed, in which case wash them with mild detergent solution.
- Glossy enamel paint can be washed with hot water. Rub gently. Remove stubborn spots with a very mild scouring powder or fine wire wool.

Linoleum

This is a natural material based on linseed oil and finely ground cork. Mop it with warm detergenty water, but don't scrub. Dry the floor thoroughly.

- Remove marks by rubbing with medium-grade steel wool dipped in turpentine.
- Remove crayon marks with a little silver polish.
- Remove grease spills by applying ice cubes immediately then removing congealed grease and washing with detergent solution.
- Polish it or seal it as for wood. If you want to use a sealant an oil-based one will bond better than a plastic-based one.

Marble

A luxury natural stone which needs very little maintenance. Use diluted washing-up liquid on a soft mop or cloth and wipe dry immediately. If there is any staining or blistering get professional advice. Don't use abrasives. Marble is porous and oils and fats will stain it while acids will pit it.

Quarry tiles

Rub tiles with linseed oil when new and don't wash them at all until two weeks after they have been laid. Damp-mop with warm detergenty water and scrub them if necessary.

- Newly laid tiles may acquire white patches which are caused by lime in the cement. Wash these in a weak solution of white vinegar and water.
- Use a silicone polish if you want to, but polish is not really necessary.
- Front steps tiled with quarry tiles are sometimes maintained with a red-coloured wax polish.

Rubber

This can be protected with a water-based sealer. Wash with detergent solution. Polish with a special rubber polish or emulsion polish. Polishes based on waxes or solvents will dissolve rubber.

Slate

Wash or scrub with a washing soda and detergent solution. Apply a little lemon juice or milk after washing to give a lustrous finish. Remove all excess with a clean cloth.

Stairs

Start from the bottom and work up. If polishing stair rods, place pieces of paper under the rods to protect the carpet.

Stone

Stone floors are porous. Mop or scrub with washing soda or detergent solution.

- Protect stone floors with a cement sealer and wax-polish thereafter.

Terrazzo

A mixture of marble chips set in cement. Mop with a washing-up liquid solution. Don't get terrazzo too wet. Dry well immediately after washing. Don't use steel wool or abrasive powders.

Thermoplastic

Mop with detergent solution and polish if you want to with a water-based emulsion polish. Don't use solvent-based cleaners or polishes as they will soften and damage the tiles.

Varnish

Mop with detergent solution. No need to polish.

Vinyl

Mop with detergent solution. Polish, if you want to, with a water-based emulsion polish. Don't use solvent-based cleaners or polishes as they will soften and damage the tiles.

- Remove crayon marks with silver polish.
- Remove grease spills by applying ice cubes immediately. When congealed, scrape up grease and clean with detergent solution.

Wood

Mop sanded and sealed floors with warm, not hot, water and detergent. Don't allow the floor to get too wet. When the seal begins to wear off, reseal it.

- Don't wash polished wood floors but after some years, when the polish has built up, you can wipe it with a cloth dipped in white vinegar and water to remove excess polish and dirt. Apply new polish sparingly and infrequently. Buff up in between. Liquid wax polish helps to remove dirt and is easier to apply than solid wax.
- If grease gets spilled, apply ice cubes immediately and then scrape the grease up and clean with detergent solution.
- Oil and grease stains can be removed with a paste of fuller's earth and soap and water. Put it on the stain and leave for two or three days to draw out the mark.
- A paste wax will also help to remove tar spots.
- Remove spilled nail varnish from waxed and shiny floors by allowing it to dry and then peeling it off. If you try and wipe it up while it is still wet you will leave smears.

CLEANING CARPETS AND SOFT FLOORCOVERINGS

On the whole we treat our carpets extraordinarily badly. We walk on them in heavy and high heeled shoes, tread mud into them, spill things on them and still expect them to last forever. If a carpet is to last it must be kept clean on a regular basis. Dust and grit are more damaging to carpets than other types of flooring since they split and cut the fibres when anyone walks over them. Anything spilled should be swept or absorbed at once.

- Occasionally (and BEFORE it actually looks grubby) give your carpet a good shampoo.

Vacuuming – the right way

The original upright vacuum cleaner which beats-as-it-sweeps-as-it-cleans is still probably the most satisfactory type for a fully carpeted home. But cylinder cleaners are more convenient for homes with a mixture of smooth floors and carpet and take up less storage space in a small home. Get one with a powerful motor, since there is no beating action to bring grit to the surface.

1 Pick up by hand all sharp, hard and ungainly objects such as nails, buttons etc as they can damage the machine.
2 Move all the furniture off the carpet.
3 Run the cleaner over each area of carpet at least 12 times, overlapping each stroke.
4 If the carpet is loose, vacuum underneath first, and then on top.

Vacuuming – the lazy way

- Just move small pieces of furniture and objects off the floor.
- Vacuum an area until it looks respectable – don't bother with 12 strokes.

Vacuuming – the green way

- Don't use perfumed vacuuming powders.
- Re-use dust bags a couple of times before throwing away.

Shampooing carpets – the right way

Check with the manufacturer before attempting to shampoo a carpet as some carpets should only be dry-cleaned. If in doubt call in a professional cleaner.

1 Remove all furniture from the room.
2 Vacuum thoroughly (see page 83).
3 Test a small piece of carpet for colour fastness (see page 38). Acetic acid or vinegar added to the shampoo may prevent the colour running.
4 Follow the instructions on the carpet shampoo pack. Use only lukewarm water. Apply gently with a soft bristle brush and don't brush synthetics too hard without enough shampoo to lubricate them or the fibres may crack or become frizzy. Treat very dirty areas twice or the end result may be patchy.
5 Vacuum again to remove dry foam and dirt and to raise the pile. Vacuum again the following day.
6 Allow the carpet to dry completely before putting the furniture back. Or put a piece of greaseproof paper or cooking foil or special plastic stands under furniture legs and castors to prevent rust stains. Don't walk on carpet while it is damp. Put brown paper or shelf paper down.
7 Brush the carpet all over in the direction of the pile. This is particularly important on cotton carpets as the pile is liable to flatten easily.

General carpet shampooing advice

• Treat stains before shampooing the carpet (see chapters 3 and 4 and page 86).
• Be sure to use a carpet shampoo not just any old detergent which may contain bleach and alkalis and would be damaging to carpets.
• A 100kg wool carpet will absorb about 16kg water before the backing becomes saturated, but 100kg synthetic carpet may absorb only about 2.5kg water before the backing is affected, so take special care not to get synthetic carpets very wet.
• Cotton takes a long time to dry out so there's more chance of mildew forming and of the colour running on cotton carpets. Dry foam shampoos are useful for these.
• If the carpet gets over-wet, fold a thick towel, place it over the wet area and stand on it. Don't rub. Wet carpets can also be suspended on bricks to allow air to circulate underneath.
• Synthetics may attract static. Use an anti-static product which will last for about 12 months. Or sprinkle the carpet very lightly with water from a fine spray nozzle because lack of moisture is the main cause of static.

Shampooing carpets – the lazy way

• Get a professional carpet cleaner in to clean the carpets for you.

Look in the Yellow Pages or write to the Textile Services Association (see Addresses) for the name of a local cleaner. If you're having a carpet professionally cleaned find out first whether the price includes moving the furniture. Some companies offer a discount if they don't have to do this. Some cleaners offer 'chemical' cleaning but this is rather drastic and not to be recommended.

- Alternatively hire a carpet cleaning machine from your local hire shop or dry-cleaners. This is worthwhile particularly if you are cleaning a lot of carpets or the carpet is very dirty. Use the machine with the recommended shampoo.
- Have a new or newly cleaned carpet treated with silicone to prevent the carpet getting dirty again too quickly and to make future cleaning easier. Treatments should last for about three years.

Shampooing carpets – the greener way

- Use the minimum amount of detergent or use a dry shampoo.
- Don't use aerosols.

CARE OF OTHER SOFT FLOORINGS

Carpet tiles

Can be lifted individually if anything gets spilled on them. If irretrievably stained, swap with unseen tile (eg one behind a door) or replace with a new one. It is useful to buy a few extra that can be slotted in if necessary.

Small cotton rugs

Machine wash.

Fur rugs

If on a felt, wool or flannel backing, clean with fuller's earth or French chalk or talcum powder: shake it over the rug and leave it for several hours then brush and shake it out.

- Wipe non-backed rugs with a cloth wrung out in lukewarm mild detergent solution.

Hooked rugs

Vacuum and sweep but don't beat or shake in case the loops become loose. Any further cleaning should be done by a professional.

Numdah rugs (embroidered Indian matted goat's hair)

Dry-clean only. Vacuum, but not with a cleaner which beats.

Door-mat, coconut, sisal, rush matting

Lift and shake out of doors and vacuum up the enormous quantity of dust that will have collected underneath. Some mats now have an impermeable backing which makes cleaning easier. If the matting is fixed, vacuum as often as you can.

STAIN REMOVAL GUIDELINES

Follow the guidelines on pages 32–52, remembering the following points:
- The secret of successful stain removal is speed – the sooner you catch the stain the better.
- Don't get the carpet too wet.
- Blot well between applications of cleaning fluid: terry towelling will absorb a good deal of moisture. Tread it into the carpet to reach the wet fibres at the bottom.
- Do not rub or brush a carpet too vigorously when cleaning.
- Remove stains before shampooing the carpet.
- Test for colour fastness before applying solvent cleaners.
- Grease, oil and tar can be cleaned with dry-cleaning solvent in a circular motion, working from the edge of the stain to the centre. Allow to dry then follow with a detergent solution, blotting between applications. Rinse well, blotting as before. Dry with a clean terry towel.
- Urine, faeces and vomit can be scraped up with a blunt knife. Then sponge with made-up carpet shampoo, adding an eggcup of white vinegar to each 600ml (1 pint), or use a proprietary spotting kit.
- Don't use detergents if you don't know what was spilled. If you do use detergent, washing-up liquid is probably as good as any.
- Certain spot removers which can safely be used on wool (ie nail varnish remover and acetone) may destroy certain acetates.
- Use acids (eg white vinegar) to remove stains from wool, camel hair, mohair and other organic or protein fibres and polyester.
- Use alkalis (eg bicarbonate of soda or a weak solution of household ammonia) on cellulose or vegetable fibres such as cotton, jute, viscose and rayon, silk and nylon.

9
Cleaning walls and ceilings

The main difficulty with cleaning walls and ceilings is their height. Make sure you have a set of sturdy steps, some absorbent cloths, a bucket of warm detergenty water and another bucket of clean rinsing water. If possible put the buckets on a chair, table or stool next to where you are working so you can reach them from your work station. The best cloths are clean floor cloths or old terry towels rather than disposable cloths which are generally not absorbent enough.

When cleaning walls near the stairs, lean a ladder against the wall with its base supported by the angle of the stair. Place a stepladder on the landing and a wide plank on one rung of the steps and one of the ladder.

WASHING PAINTWORK – THE RIGHT WAY

Walls

For very dirty walls, or before repainting, use a sugar soap solution, otherwise use a mild detergent solution.

1 Squeeze out a sponge or cloth in detergent solution. You need just enough to get at the dirt, not enough to run down the wall (or your shirtsleeve) in streaks.
2 Start at the top and work down. Work on one reachable section at a time. Sponge or wipe the area with detergent.
3 When you have covered a section, go back to the beginning with a clean cloth wrung out in clean water and wipe off detergent and dirt.
• If the walls are very dirty, allow the detergent a little longer to get at the dirt before wiping it off.

- Change the water in the bucket frequently.
- On gloss walls, give a final wipe with a clean, dry terry towel to remove any detergent streaks on the paint.

Ceilings

If the ceiling has yellowed with smoke, age, water stains, fluorescent tube marks etc, slap a coat of emulsion paint on. This is easier and more effective than trying to wash the ceiling. If you must clean it, use a clean, dry broom rather than a wet cloth. Take down light fittings and clean them at the same time.

- Acoustic tile ceilings can be cleaned with a dry sponge once a year.
- Cover small marks on white ceilings with a dab of white shoe polish.
- If you must wash a ceiling, work on 1 metre (3 foot) square sections at a time using the same method given for walls. Cover the floor with polythene sheeting to catch splatters of detergent solution. Wear goggles.

Washing paintwork – the lazy way

- Use a clean sponge floor mop to reach the top of the wall instead of setting up a ladder.
- If you were thinking of it, don't clean the insides of wardrobes and cupboards. When clearing out at spring cleaning time, give them a brush with a clean broom, otherwise leave them alone.
- If your walls are cleanish, forget about the two buckets mentioned above and just wipe the walls over with a cloth wrung out in warm water with a little white vinegar added.

Washing paintwork – the green way

- Use a weaker solution of detergent with a little white vinegar added or use just water and vinegar.

CLEANING WALLCOVERINGS

Brick

- Brush and vacuum and pull out all loose grit.
- Untreated bricks are best left to acquire a natural patina of grime, and washing them will usually make any marks worse.
- Sealed bricks can be washed with detergent solution.

Ceramic tiles and gloss paints

1   Wipe with a cloth wrung out in soapless detergent. A sponge mop works well on tiled walls and a squeegee is also useful for very dirty walls.

2   Wipe with a clean sponge squeezed in clean water.

3   Remove stains with paste cleaner or a nylon pad.

- Car wax is a good tile cleanser and polish. Rub it in with a soft cloth, leave for 10 minutes, but don't allow it to dry completely. Polish with a soft cloth.
- Discoloured grout should be rubbed with a toothbrush and proprietary bathroom cleaner or half and half solution of household bleach or liquid antiseptic and water. It may be easier to re-grout though, or paint with special grout paint (available in a range of colours).
- For a green way to clean ceramic tiles rub with a cut lemon. Leave for 15 minutes, then polish with a soft, dry cloth.

Embossed wallpapers

A soft toothbrush will get dust out of valleys.

Fabric and cork

- Dust or vacuum with the dusting attachment of your machine.
- Pat with a damp cloth wrung out in warm water. Test a small patch first to check that the colours won't run.
- Felt should be given a 'dry shampoo'. Spread bran, fuller's earth or talcum powder on to the wall. Leave for a few hours and then vacuum. Cover the floor with a groundsheet or plastic sheeting because you are bound to spill a good deal. Test a small piece first. Vacuuming may pull the felt from the wall, so you might have to pat it to release the powder instead.
- Cork can be sealed with a matt seal and washed as for washable wallcoverings. If it is not sealed, don't try to wash it, just keep it well dusted.

Lacquered wallpapers

Use warm detergent solution and wash as for walls.

Mouldings

- Check that mouldings are, indeed, washable and that any chips and cracks won't be further damaged by the water. Don't wash plaster mouldings, which will smudge and streak. Paint them instead, when you next paint the ceiling.
- Dust with a cobweb brush or a feather duster on a long handle.
- If mouldings are very dirty, spray with detergent solution in a spray bottle with a fine spray. Wait for the liquid to penetrate then wipe with a dry cloth and spray again with clear water.
- Terry towelling is good for mouldings because the loops of thread mop up water in the crevices.

Non-washable wallcoverings

- Brush occasionally with a cobweb brush or broom.
- Pat stubborn marks lightly with a damp cloth. Gently pat the paper dry. Don't rub.
- Proprietary cleaners are available of modelling-dough texture which can be used to gently erase stains. Or use a soft eraser or lumps of bread. Use them with a downward sweeping movement. Don't press too hard and don't rub sideways. None of these will remove marks on very dirty walls or get rid of crayon marks and they may themselves leave streaky marks.

Washable papers

These are not really 'washable' but can be sponged gently with mild white soap suds applied on a soft sponge and patted dry with a clean cloth.

Washable wallcoverings (textured vinyl etc)

- Dust frequently because dirt tends to make the wallcovering brittle.
- If necessary wipe with detergent solution on a cloth or sponge. You can use dry-cleaning solvents on stains. Don't use lacquer solvents which will damage the surface.

Wood panelling

- Waxed or sealed panels just need dusting and the occasional wipe with a sponge wrung out in liquid detergent solution.
- Varnished or lacquered wood should be cleaned with furniture polish.
- Painted panels can be cleaned with detergent solution on a soft cloth or sponge. Don't use abrasive cleaners, wire wool etc.
- Touch up discoloured panelling with shoe polish, dark wax polish or proprietary wood stain. BE CAREFUL. If you make it too dark you can't then lighten it again.

Removing specific stains

If the method of stain removal is going to do a lot of damage to the wall covering, it may be best to live with a mark until you next re-decorate.

Ball-point pen

- On paint use methylated spirit. You can try this on wallcoverings as well, but don't rub too hard for fear of damaging the finish.
- On walls try using a soft nail brush or old toothbrush.
- On cork you can try the method above, but it may not work.

- On wood panelling try mild detergent solution, followed by methylated spirits on cotton wool. But almost any treatment will discolour the wood so you may have to use shoe polish or wood stain to bring it back to its correct colour.
- On brick or new plaster use paint remover and give it time to work on the marks before you scrape it off. Wash with detergent solution. If necessary use fine grade sandpaper.

Crayon

- On paintwork try a dough ball or an eraser (see page 89).
- On most wallcoverings draw out the wax with a warm iron over blotting paper or kitchen tissues, which will absorb it. Any residual stain may be rubbed with white spirit or moistened bicarbonate of soda on a damp cloth.
- On brick, use paint remover and give it time to work on the marks before you scrape it off. Wash with detergent solution. If necessary, use sandpaper.

Fingermarks

These may respond to a little diluted washing-up liquid rubbed gently in and then rinsed off thoroughly. Rub the mark only and not the surrounding area.

Grease

- On paint rub with strong detergent solution with a little white spirit added.
- On washable and unwashable wallcoverings draw out the grease with blotting paper or kitchen tissues under a warm iron. Or apply a paste of fuller's earth and dry-cleaning fluid, allow it to dry and then brush it off.

- On embossed wallcoverings dab with talcum powder, leave for a couple of hours then brush off gently.
- On vinyl dab with dry-cleaning solvent and then detergent solution, then clean water.
- On cork dab with water containing borax or a mild detergent solution with a few drops of household ammonia.
- On silk, get professional advice.
- On wood panelling use a mild detergent solution followed by white spirit on cotton wool.
- On brick, sponge with white spirit.

Sticky tape

- Masking tape and other adhesive tapes should be peeled off while still fresh. If it has been on for some time, it can be difficult to remove. Peel off carefully so you don't leave part of the tape on the wall or tear the wallcovering. Use acetone or non-oily nail varnish remover to soften the glue base. Acetone and nail varnish remover will damage some paints and some plastic surfaces so don't leave them on too long.
- Remove sticky tape by lifting the top edge and pulling it back on itself, keeping it parallel with the wall and pulling slowly and evenly. It may help to play a hair dryer along it, allowing the warmth to soften the glue.
- Old collages or transfers may come off if you paint them with several coats of white vinegar. Give it time to soak in and then wash the pictures off. Or let a few drops of oil soak into the stuck paper. Rub gently with a soft cloth.

10
Cleaning windows and plate glass

The difference between looking through clean and dirty windows is amazing. Clean and polish them inside and out and you'll wonder why you didn't do it sooner. House plants will benefit too.

Cleaning windows can be an irritating chore, however, especially if water drips down your arms or the smears just won't come off. Most people tend to use too much detergent in the water when cleaning windows, which results in streaks. One capful of detergent in a bucket of warm water is enough. Many professionals insist that they use just cool, clean water, which is fine for moderately clean windows. But these are just two of the many ways you can clean windows.

CLEANING WINDOWS – THE RIGHT WAY

Equipment

1   You will need one of the following:
    - a proprietary window cleaning product.
    - a bucket of weak detergent solution (see above).
    - between 1 teaspoon and an eggcupful of vinegar in a bucket of warm water.
    - simply a bucket of tepid, not hot, water.
    - a mixture of equal parts of methylated spirits, paraffin and water. Put into a bottle and shake hard and often.
    - a mixture of ½ cup ammonia, 1 cup white vinegar, and 2 tablespoons cornflour in a bucket of tepid water.
2   Bucket of clean, warm water, to rinse the cloth in from time to time.

- On cold days add ½ cup of white spirit to each litre (2 pints) of water to prevent it freezing on the glass – although it's not advisable to wash windows when it is this cold.
3   Squeegee (a rubber strip in a holder on the end of a handle) to clean the window.
4   Non-linty cloths to apply the solution and to wipe the squeegee with.
5   Chamois, scrim or newspaper to buff up the glass after washing and give a good shine.
6   A sturdy pair of steps, not just a chair.

Tips for success

- Clean windows when the sun is NOT shining on them.
- Don't clean windows on a frosty day when the glass is more brittle and may break.
- Clean windows often so that cleaning is easy. Don't let them get really dirty which will result in a waste of your time and effort.
- Change the water frequently.
- Use all detergents etc sparingly or they will cause streaks.
- Use crossways strokes for inside, vertical strokes for outside so that you can see which side the smears are on.
- Proprietary window cleaners are for use on dry windows. Don't use them on windows covered in condensation droplets or on windows you have already made wet with a water or detergent solution.
- Don't use a dry cloth on a dirty window or you'll scratch the glass.

Large windows

1   Take down blinds, curtains and all objects on the window sill.
2   Clean frames round windows before starting on the glass.
3   Wipe the top of the window with a cloth squeezed out in cleaning mixture.
4   Use a squeegee to wipe across the top of the window bringing the edge down so that you get right into the corners and sides of the glass.
5   Wipe the squeegee blade on the cloth after each stroke.
6   When you have squeegeed the wet part of the window, continue wiping with the cloth and then the squeegee until you reach the bottom.
7   Wipe the cleaned window with scrim, a chamois or crumpled newspapers to give it a final shine. If you have such a thing, use a blackboard eraser for extra shine.

Small window panes

1   Take down blinds, curtains and all objects on the window sill.
2   Clean window frames with detergent solution, before starting on the glass.
3   If using proprietary cleaner, follow the instructions. If you are using a home-made mixture, squeeze out the cloth in the bucket of mixture, wringing it out well.
4   Work round the edges of each pane and into the middle.
5   Wipe with a clean cloth squeezed out in the clean water immediately. Don't wait for it to dry.
•   Small panes in a glazed bookcase should be dusted and wiped with a very little methylated spirit or white spirit on cotton wool. Use a circular motion. Change the cotton wool as soon as it is dirty.

Cleaning windows – the lazy way

•   Leave out the final buff with the scrim, chamois or newspaper.
•   Small panes can usually be left for longer between washes as they don't show the dirt as much as large ones.
•   Don't become obsessive about small marks left on the glass when you've finished cleaning. You won't get rid of them by wiping at them individually and they won't show to anyone else. This is the sensible way, not just the lazy way.

Cleaning windows – the green way

•   Don't use aerosols of any kind.
•   Use any proprietary window cleaners and detergents very sparingly indeed.
•   For preference use the vinegar and water mixture.
•   Fly spots can be removed with cold tea.

GENERAL WINDOW CLEANING ADVICE

•   Don't try to clean windows which are difficult to reach or above first floor level.
•   Don't hold the bucket while cleaning and don't perch it on a window ledge.
•   It can be useful to have a squeegee with an extended angle handle.
•   Don't waste money on gimmicky window cleaners, such as magnetic ones, which don't really work.
•   Remove fresh paint marks with turpentine, dry-cleaning solvent or nail varnish remover on a non-linty cloth.
•   Soften dried paint splodges with turpentine or white spirit.

- Remove putty marks with ammonia or soften them with turpentine or white spirit.
- Don't use any abrasives to clean window glass.
- For very dirty windows add a small amount of washing-up liquid or borax to the washing mixture.
- Remove sticky labels or their adhesive with methylated or white spirit on cotton wool.
- Remove flyscreens before cleaning the windows and brush them with the vacuum cleaner attachment or with a stiff bristle brush.

Other types of glass

Glass shower screens

Get rid of soap and water marks by rubbing with a sponge dipped in white vinegar.

Glass table tops

Clean as for small panes, or try with a squeegee. Use vinegar and water, or lemon juice, or white spirit, or any of the mixtures for window cleaning (see page 93).

- Rub fingermarks on clean glass with a cloth dipped in neat vinegar.
- Remove sticky label or tape marks by rubbing with a little peanut butter then wiping off.

Mirrors

Clean with a soft cloth just dampened with any of the mixtures suggested for window cleaning. Take care not to get water between the mirror and frame or into the backing. The cloth should only be damp, not wet. Finish off with a clean chamois or lint-free cloth.

Painted glass

Don't wash painted glass. Dust it with a very soft paintbrush instead.

Sliding glass doors

Wrap a small cloth round an eraser to get rid of track marks on the glass.

Stained-glass panes

Modern stained glass is usually quite robust. Clean it as for small window panes.

- Antique panes should be washed very gently. Don't use commercial products or detergent.

11
Cleaning furniture and upholstery

Little and often is the best advice for cleaning furniture and upholstery. Dusting and vacuuming and the immediate removal of anything spilled are the things which will do most to give your furniture a longer life and a fresher appearance. When using cleaners and polishes be very sparing, and when vacuuming be very gentle, especially on upholstery fabrics.

WOODEN FURNITURE

All polished, waxed and untreated woods need regular cleaning to keep them in good condition. The right way, the lazy way and the green way to treat wood are the same if you avoid aerosol sprays and use only natural furniture polishes like beeswax.

Dusting

Dust polished furniture frequently. Regular and thorough dusting is the most important treatment for good wooden furniture. Take care to remove the dust and not just move it about. Use a clean duster and shake it outside afterwards. Don't forget to dust all round the legs, dowels and feet.
- Don't use a feather duster on valuable furniture because broken feathers can scratch the surface.

Polishing

Polish does not actually penetrate or feed the wood. It protects the surface and gives it an attractive finish. The resulting shine also makes it easier to dust. So when applying any sort of polish it is important to make the coating as thin as possible to show up the wood grain and to prevent a build-up of wax which will attract dust.

1   Before polishing, you can remove any build-up of old polish with white vinegar on a damp cloth.
2   Greasy marks can be removed with a chamois wrung out in a mixture of 1 tablespoon vinegar in 300ml (½ pint) water.
3   Apply polish sparingly on a soft cloth and polish off straight away with a clean cloth.

• Don't use modern furniture creams on antique pieces because these products contain an emulsifying agent which may harm the wood.
• Synthetic furniture polishes are based on silicones which are not an environmental hazard in themselves but the synthetic solvents and perfumes that they contain often are.
• Don't use aerosols; apart from the environmental reasons, the solvent comes out with such force that it can damage the polished surface. Where such polishes have been used a lot, the furniture aquires a milky look for which there is no cure.

French polish

French polish was introduced into England around 1820. The technique involves applying shellac dissolved in methylated spirit and the wood should look satiny rather than mirror-shiny.

1   Dust. Don't use oiled or treated dusters.
2   Remove sticky marks with a cloth wrung out in warm detergent solution or with a cloth dipped in white vinegar.
3   Polish very occasionally using a small amount of furniture cream or wax polish.

• If alcohol is spilled on a French polished surface it will remove the polish. Take prompt action by wiping it up immediately then rubbing the area with the palm of your hand. This is slightly oily and will help to replace some of the wax.

Wax-polished furniture

This is created by scrubbing the wood with a mixture of wax, turpentine and colouring, then painstakingly polishing it. The result is a very rich, deep shine.

• Treat as for French polished furniture. Use a clean duster and uncoloured polish.
• Oak and mahogany may be rubbed with a cloth dipped in warm beer.

Untreated wood

Untreated solid wood is sometimes used for kitchen worktops. Maple and mahogany are popular. There are also untreated teak and deal tables for kitchens.

1 Wipe over the surface with a cloth dipped in white vinegar to remove surface dirt but don't leave the surface wet.

2 Apply a thin coating of teak oil or linseed oil to hardwood tops using a cloth and rubbing along the grain. This will prevent the wood from drying out and protect it from dampness, stains etc. Do this only about once every six months. Teak and linseed oil are flammable so work away from naked flames and throw away the cloth after use.

• Scrub deal tables with a clean scrubbing brush and a detergent solution.

Some special cases

Cane, wicker and bamboo furniture

This should be brushed and vacuumed regularly as dust collects in the weave.

• Scrub with a solution of salt and water if necessary, then rinse well. Don't use detergent. Dry in the sun if possible.

• Polish with furniture cream if necessary.

Carved wood

• Dust with a dry decorator's dusting brush, a watercolour brush or an oil-paint brush.

• Get into crevices with a soft toothbrush. This is also useful for removing polish which has lodged in there.

Gilded finishes

The wood is treated to give the impression of gold.

• Don't let water anywhere near gilding.

• Dust gently using a dry watercolour paintbrush. Don't rub.

• Clean with a soft cloth lightly dipped in warm turpentine or white spirit. (Because these spirits are flammable, warm them by standing the bottle in a bowl of hot water rather than letting them anywhere near a naked flame or direct heat.)

• Remove stains by gently dabbing with half a raw onion.

• If any piece of gilt seems to be flaking off, get professional advice.

• Don't try to retouch any true gilding yourself. Never be tempted to touch up with gold paint as it is a completely different colour and will give a different effect.

Lacquered or Japanned furniture

Keep in a dry balanced temperature as it will suffer in temperature changes and damp atmospheres.
- Wipe down with a damp cloth.
- Remove fingermarks with a damp chamois leather and buff up gently with a soft duster.
- Occasionally polish surfaces with wax polish.

Polyurethane finish

A tough finish.
- Just wipe over with a damp cloth.

Veneered wood and marquetry

Treat carefully to avoid damaging delicate inlay.
- Dust very carefully using a duster with no frayed edges or loose threads which could catch in the inlays and leave tufts behind or even pull pieces of veneer away.
- Polish with a little furniture cream or wax polish depending on the type of wood and finish.
- Mop up water spills immediately and don't allow the wood to get wet with any cleaning solution.
- Don't polish pieces of wood which are damaged or lifting; if wax gets under them, it will then be impossible to glue them back into place should you ever have the item repaired.
- While cleaning, check the surfaces for any bubbling or damage.

Wooden garden furniture

This is usually made of cedar or other hardwoods. The wood is designed to weather and looks best when it has weathered a bit.
- Wipe with a chamois or cloth wrung out in warm water. Rinse with cold water and dry.
- Remove stains by rubbing gently with fine wire wool along the grain. Don't use abrasives or scrub as though you were dealing with a kitchen table.

Remedial treatments for waxed and polished furniture

Don't treat valuable furniture yourself, get a professional to do it.

Black water marks

Rub the surface with fine steel wool then re-colour and repolish.
- Or bleach with a proprietary wood bleach.

Cigarette burns

Treat as for white rings (see below).
- If necessary lightly sandpaper the area and build it up again with coloured beeswax. Do not do this on valuable antiques.

Dents

Fill small dents by melting equal parts of beeswax and resin in a double saucepan. While still pliable fill the hole with the mixture and when dry, smooth with fine sandpaper, taking care not to damage the rest of the wood.

Ink stains

Try a proprietary wood bleach.

Scratches

Conceal light scratches by rubbing them with the kernel of a Brazil nut. This works with lightning speed.
- Or rub them with a proprietary furniture renovator, working in the direction of the grain.
- Or pour cod liver oil on and leave to soak in.

White frosting

This can sometimes be caused by a damp environment. It may cover the whole surface, but probably won't penetrate the wood.
- Dip a piece of fine steel wool into cooking oil and rub along the grain. Finish with a wax polish.

White rings

These may be caused by water or heat.
- Rub gently with a paste of salt and cooking oil on a soft cloth. Polish with a soft, dry cloth.
- Or rub with very fine steel wool and olive oil in the direction of the grain.
- Or apply a paste of mayonnaise, or olive oil and cigarette ash. Leave for a while, then remove the paste and buff up with a damp cloth.
- Or rub with metal polish along the grain. Buff up with a soft cloth.

LAMINATED PLASTIC FURNITURE

Clean carefully as it is easily scratched.
- Wipe laminated furniture with a cloth wrung out in a mild detergent solution. Don't use abrasives, chemical cleaners or ammonia.

- Rub light stains with a damp cloth dipped in bicarbonate of soda.
- Rub stubborn stains with toothpaste or cover them in a paste of bicarbonate of soda and water and leave for several hours. Then rub briskly before wiping off.

Acrylic furniture
Wipe with a mild detergent solution.
- Rub scratches with metal polish.

CLEANING UPHOLSTERY – THE RIGHT WAY

As with all fabrics, the more regularly you clean upholstery, the easier it will be. Accumulations of surface dirt, dust, perspiration, hair oil and so on will damage the fibres – and so will the rigorous cleaning you have to give to really grubby textiles.

General rules

- Vacuum cushions, arm rests, backs and crevices every week.
- Pat upholstery gently with a plastic fly-swat or old fashioned carpet beater to loosen the dust before vacuuming.
- Mop up anything spilled at once, before it stains the fabric. Many things are quite easy to get rid of at the time, but impossible later on. Treat according to the stain and type of fabric. See chapters 3 and 4.
- Turn cushions occasionally so that they wear evenly. Shampoo chairs and seats two or three times a year.
- Don't vacuum fringes or embroidery or anything with beads or sequins on.
- Don't use a vacuum with extra strong suction. A small, hand-held vacuum is the best type for cleaning upholstery.
- Don't use the brush attachments when vacuuming.

Shampooing upholstery

1   Remove as much surface dirt as possible with a thorough vacuuming, getting into all corners and crevices and working on the seams and piping etc.
2   Spot clean stains at this stage if you didn't do it at the time they were made (see chapters 3 and 4).
3   Choose a cleaning product suitable for the upholstery fabric. Otherwise, your usual carpet shampoo may be suitable, but use just the foam so as not to get the upholstery too wet.

4   Whatever product you are using, follow the manufacturer's instructions. Test the fabric for colour-fastness in an inconspicuous area. Treat it with a little of the upholstery shampoo, leave it for a short while and then dab it with tissues. If no colour comes off onto the tissue, go ahead with the shampooing. If colour does come off, either shampoo with great care or get the piece professionally cleaned.

5   Treat a small area at a time, using as little water and cleaning fluid as possible, so the padding doesn't get wet.

6   For robust fabrics rub the entire surface vigorously with a damp (not wet) towel to take off the foam residue and loosened dirt. A Turkish towel which is both rough and absorbent is excellent. Don't rub delicate fabrics. Blot them instead with clean white tissues.

7   Blot with tepid water to rinse. Dry with a Turkish towel and don't get the fabric too wet.

8   Allow to dry, then vacuum thoroughly again.

•   If, after shampooing, there are still stains, treat with dry-cleaning solvent.

Cleaning upholstery – the lazy way

Dry foam upholstery shampoos are the easiest to use as they dry to form crystals, drawing out the dirt as they dry. The crystals are then vacuumed away. Rub obstinate stains with the applicator brush or a soft toothbrush. Don't brush delicate fabrics. Use a sponge instead.

•   Or have the upholstery professionally cleaned.
•   Have new or newly cleaned upholstery treated with a stain guard process to prevent it soiling too quickly.
•   Arm caps and head rest covers will protect the areas most quickly soiled.
•   Or use removable stretch covers. It is easier to remove these and wash them than to shampoo the upholstery in situ.

Cleaning upholstery – the green way

•   Avoid aerosol shampoos and stain removers.
•   Use the minimum amount of detergent and don't mix more than you need.
•   After shampooing treat any residual stains with a detergent solution containing 1 teaspoon of white vinegar.

Some special cases

Cushions

These can have removable or non-removable covers.

- Take off and wash removable cushion covers fairly frequently.
- If using upholstery shampoo or dry-cleaning fluids on non-removable covers don't get the fillings too wet.
- Don't wash feather-filled cushions or the feathers will poke out of the fabric.
- Don't wash kapok as it will go lumpy.

Leather upholstery

Dust or vacuum regularly.

- Clean dirty areas with saddle soap, using as little water as possible. When dry, buff up with a soft cloth.
- Rub dark leather every six months or so with castor oil or neat's foot oil to prevent the leather from cracking. Clean the leather first. Apply a small amount of oil with a cotton wool pad or the fingertips. Rub it in well and take off any surplus.
- Rub pale leather with petroleum jelly.
- Don't wax leather furniture as it won't absorb the wax. You can use a little shoe cream instead if you wish, but make sure you rub it in well and polish off any excess so that it doesn't get transferred to your clothes.
- Sometimes hide begins to get a dried-out look, especially in centrally heated homes. Apply a proprietary hide food with swabs of cotton wool. Leave for 24 hours for the leather to absorb it, then buff up with a soft, clean duster.
- Or sponge with vinegar and water with a little ammonia added. While still wet apply castor oil on a rag. When the leather is dry polish with furniture cream.
- When using any sort of leather renovator be careful not to touch any embossed gilding and keep the product away from any surrounding wood.

Loose covers

- Wash stretch covers at home in the machine.
- Larger cotton and linen covers are too cumbersome for most domestic machines and are difficult to dry at home anyway, so take them to the launderette or send to the laundry.
- Iron on the wrong side so the fabric doesn't go shiny. However, loose covers are difficult to iron because they are so ungainly and bulky. This is another good reason for sending them to the laundry.

Plastic and vinyl

Use a proprietary vinyl car-seat cleaner to clean vinyl upholstery.
- Wipe sticky marks with a mild soap and water solution. Don't use detergent.

Tapestry and embroidery

Valuable needlepoint or worn tapestry should be dealt with by experts.
- Vacuum needlepoint once a week using low suction and don't give it any other treatment at all. Don't rub the surface hard, just keep the vacuum head close enough to the fabric to pick up dust.
- Don't vacuum embroidery. Instead cover with warm bran, leave for several hours then shake off.
- Embroidery and other delicate fabrics can be brushed very gently with a baby's hairbrush.

12
A-Z of household objects and materials

This is a quick reference chapter for items round the home which may not fit into another category or which need special treatment. If you look for an item here and don't find it, clean according to the material it is made of.

Acrylic plastics and fibreglass

Clean with warm detergent solution. Don't use abrasives. Don't use dry-cleaning solvents.
• Scratches can be concealed by polishing with a little metal polish.

Alabaster

Similar to marble. Often made into lamp bases and ornaments. Treat as for marble and be sure not to let liquid soak in because alabaster is porous.

Antiques

Care of antiques should be the same as for anything of similar materials except that you should treat the object with extreme respect, handle it ultra gently and if you are in any doubt about how to treat it or what it is made of, or if it is damaged, take it to a professional.

Artificial flowers

Pour salt into a large paper bag. Put the flowers in, heads down. Shake vigorously. The dirt will be transferred to the salt.
• Many artificial flowers can be washed. Check when buying. Dunk them up and down in a bowl of warm water and mild detergent. Rinse in the same way.

Ash trays

Tip out all debris into the rubbish bin. Wash the ash tray (separately from the rest of the washing up) in warm, detergenty water. Then clean according to the material it is made of.

Baking tins

Don't try to keep baking tins bright and shining, they take up the heat better when they are matt and dull.

- Wash in detergent and water and dry thoroughly.
- To remove burned-on food boil the tin for three to five minutes in water to which a little bicarbonate of soda has been added. Alternatively soak the tins for several hours in detergent and water and wash them later.
- To remove rust marks rub with a piece of cut raw potato dipped in flour or a mild abrasive.

Baskets

Vacuum thoroughly and frequently. Give them a good scrub with warm water about once a year, or play the garden hose on them to prevent the cane from drying out and splitting. Dry thoroughly, preferably in the sun.

Baths

See page 74.

Books

Dust with the dusting brush of a vacuum cleaner or with a clean, soft, slightly damp paintbrush or make-up brush. Take each book off the shelf and dust outwards from the binding. It is OK to flip the pages to dust them, but don't bang them together.

- A centrally heated atmosphere is not good for books as it damages the backings, pages and bindings. Dampness on the other hand will cause mildew. If you have central heating, a humidifier in the room where the books are kept would help. Even a bowl of water will provide a little moisture in the atmosphere.
- Valuable antique books should be cleaned by a professional.
- Use saddle soap occasionally on leather bindings. Spread the dressing quickly with your fingers or the palm of your hand or use a small piece of chamois, felt or muslin. Be sparing and be careful not to touch the paper or cloth parts of the book. Massage it in gently until the soap has been absorbed. The leather will almost certainly be slightly darkened by this treatment but in centrally heated homes, particularly, it is a wise precaution to stop the leather drying out.
- If moulds begin to form on books move them from the damp atmosphere, or dry out the room. Fresh moulds can be wiped off the bindings with a clean, soft cloth.

- Mildew on pages can be wiped off in the same way.
- Or slightly dampen the cloth with white spirit and spread the pages fanwise to dry.
- Or dust the mildewed pages with cornflour, French chalk, bran, fuller's earth or talcum powder. Leave the powder in the closed book for several days, then brush it off.
- Books which have been left in the damp or damaged by flood should be treated bit by bit. Put sheets of tissue paper or blotting paper between the pages. Put a weight on top and leave in warm, dry air or in a room with a fan heater directed towards them but not too close.
- Remove grease spots from a page by putting a piece of blotting paper on either side of the page and pressing gently with a warm iron.

Bottles

Fill with detergent and water and wash with a bottle brush.
- Babies' bottles should be cleaned with a proprietary sterilising kit according to the manufacturer's instructions.

Brooms and dustpan brushes

Wash in warm water and mild detergent with a little washing-soda if they are very dirty. Then rinse a couple of times. If the broom is nylon or plastic, soak for five minutes in a bucket of water with 30g (2 tablespoons) of kitchen salt dissolved in it to stiffen the bristles.

Candlesticks

Don't use a knife to scrape off the wax. Pour warm water into the candle holder to soften the old wax so you can remove it more easily. To remove wax from the outer surface, push it off gently with a soft cloth wrapped around your finger.
- Don't stand weighted or hollow candlesticks in water.

Chandeliers

Dust frequently and clean them according to the material they are made of. Switch the electricity off at the mains. Unscrew every light bulb and clean each individually. While cleaning, check that the ceiling fixture and chain are in good condition.
- Wipe each pendant with cotton-gloved fingers dipped in a solution of vinegar and water or methylated spirits and water.
- The lazy way to clean crystal chandeliers is to hold a tumbler of hot water and vinegar up to each pendant until it is immersed and then allow it to drip dry. Put a dust sheet or polythene sheet underneath to catch the drips.

China, porcelain and pottery

Wash earthenware by machine (if dishwasher proof) or hand wash in clean hot water and washing-up liquid.

- Wash fine china by hand in a plastic bowl to prevent chipping. Rinse and dry. Don't soak or rub hard or use cleaning powders or scourers which will damage the glaze and the pattern.
- Cracks in fine porcelain can often be made less obvious by removing the dirt. Cover the crack with a cotton wool pad soaked in a solution of household ammonia or chlorine bleach. Leave it for several days, wetting the pad from time to time with more solution. Scrub gently if necessary with a fine-bristle brush dipped in the solution.
- Don't pour cold water over hot china or hot water over cold china in case they crack or break due to the sudden change in temperature.
- Fine china, kept for display, should only be wiped over occasionally first with a damp cloth and then a dry one.
- China with a raised pattern can be cleaned with an eyebrow or make-up brush kept for the purpose.
- Get rid of tea and coffee stains from china mugs, cups and teapots by rubbing them with a soft wet cloth dipped in bicarbonate of soda. There are some proprietary products for removing these stains, but bicarbonate is cheaper and greener.
- Earthenware, stoneware and salt-glaze ware are tougher than fine china, and often ovenproof and won't be harmed by boiling water or soaking. They can be washed satisfactorily in a dishwasher.
- Do not wash unglazed pottery. Just wipe with a damp cloth. Partially glazed bowls and dishes should be washed quickly by hand and not soaked.
- Check that china is dishwasher proof before putting it in your machine.
- Soaking old china in water may soften the colour and is specially damaging to any gold decoration.
- For general advice on washing-up see Chapter 7.

Cloisonné

This is a form of enamelling in which each part of the design is outlined by bits of wire. Wash it as you would a piece of fine china, with mild detergent and water. Rinse. Wipe dry with a soft cloth. Don't use abrasives or harsh cleaners.

Clothes pegs

Wooden pegs can be machine washed in a cotton bag or pillow case. Nylon pegs should be hand washed in a bowl of hot washing-up liquid.

Coffee-maker

Wash the inside every time you use the machine or traces of oil from the last brew will give the new one a bitter taste. Wipe the outside with a cloth wrung out in detergenty water.

- If there's an electric element don't get it wet.
- Don't tip coffee grounds down the drain. They will eventually clog it up, as will tea leaves.

Combs

Soak for a few minutes in 1 dessertspoonful of household ammonia to 600ml (1 pint) of warm water. Wash with a nailbrush. Rinse well. Dry away from heat.

Coral

See Jewellery.

Corks

Sterilise in boiling water. Other cork objects, ice boxes for instance, can be rubbed with fine emery paper or emery cloth.

Cutlery

See pages 71–2, 113 and 128.

Decanters

See Glass.

Diamonds

See Jewellery.

Dustbins and pedal bins

Line all bins with plastic or paper liners. Remove the liners and seal them up before they beome too full. This will keep the bin much cleaner and you will have to wash it less often.

- The greener way is to wrap rubbish in old newspaper and put it in the unlined bin.
- Wash the bin with hot detergent solution, using a little disinfectant if it is needed. Dry and air well.
- Grind half a lemon in a food processor and put it in the dustbin to counteract unpleasant smells.

Electric blankets and heating pads

Electric blankets should be checked for safety by the manufacturer every year. Wash or clean them according to the manufacturer's instructions. Don't use dry-cleaning solvents, which might damage

the insulation wires. Some laundries specialise in cleaning such
blankets.
- Don't use mothproofers on electric blankets because they may
  damage the wiring.
- Store in a plastic bag.

Washable electric blankets If you hand wash a blanket, shake it
gently and soak it for 10–15 minutes in tepid water and mild
detergent. Squeeze the suds gently through the fabric from time to
time. Rinse two or three times in the same way. Do not wring or
twist.
- If using a washing machine, fill the machine first with tepid
  water and agitate to dissolve the detergent. Then soak the
  blanket without tumbling for 15–20 minutes. Rinse in the same
  way. Gently pull the blanket into shape and hang to dry.

Electric heaters

Dust will make your heater less efficient and more expensive to run.
Disconnect the electricity when dusting, cleaning or polishing. If the
heater has a fan, oil it every six months. Keep any reflectors brightly
polished.

Emeralds

See Jewellery.

Enamel pots and pans

Enamel is a tough finish produced by fusing a special kind of glass
onto a metal base. For cooking pans, baths etc the base is cast iron or
steel. For jewellery it may be silver or gold (see Jewellery). Enamel
can be chipped quite easily and sudden changes of temperature may
crack it so cold pans should be heated slowly and hot pans should not
be put down on a cold surface or filled with cold water.
- Wash enamel plates, bowls, mugs etc in warm water and
  detergent. Do not use metal scrapers or scouring powders or
  anything abrasive. If food is stuck to the enamel, soak it in water
  for a few hours.
- You can safely use a nylon scourer on pans. If the food is burned
  on hard, fill the pan with water, add a couple of teaspoons of
  bicarbonate of soda and boil. Rinse and dry.
- Enamel does not like acid so don't let tomatoes, rhubarb, citrus
  fruits or other acid foods sit in an enamel pan.
- Light stains can often be removed by rubbing the enamel with a
  damp cloth dipped in bicarbonate of soda. Rinse and dry.

Glassware

- Add an eggcupful of white vinegar to washing-up water to make glasses sparkle.
- Hot white vinegar will remove paint spots from glass.

Decanters, carafes and narrow-necked vases There are several methods of cleaning green mould, watermarks and other stains which are difficult to remove from narrow-necked containers.
1 Shake tea-leaves and vinegar in the vase together. Rinse and dry.
2 Fill with water plus 2 teaspoons household ammonia. Stand overnight. Wash and rinse.
3 Fill with a little sea sand or fine aquarium gravel with a squeeze of washing-up liquid and warm water. Shake well. Leave for a few minutes, shake again. Carry on until the sediment is loose.

Hairbrushes

Wash regularly in warm detergenty water. Brushes with nylon backs and nylon bristles can be boiled. Rinse well and dry away from direct heat.

Handbags

Keep handbags filled with crumpled newspaper when not in use to retain their shape.
Leather Clean handles with saddle soap and then rub with leather conditioner. Polish briskly with a soft cloth.
- Use coloured shoe polishes to restore colour in worn areas.
Patent leather and suede See Shoes.
Plastic and vinyl Wipe with a mild soap and water solution or use a proprietary vinyl car-seat cleaner.
Linings Sprinkle with fuller's earth or bran. Leave it to absorb the dirt and then vacuum or brush it out well. Or wipe the lining with a cloth wrung out in detergenty water and allow to dry naturally.

Hinges

All hinges should be checked and oiled from time to time. Remove dirt with a small clean paintbrush then smear with petroleum jelly working it into the joints (use a swab of cotton wool on a matchstick). This should stop squeaks and rusting. Remove surplus with paper tissues.

Hot water bottles

Rubber-ridged and fabric-covered hot water bottles may be soaked for two or three minutes in hot water and mild liquid detergent. Scrub with a soft nail brush or a sponge.

- The outside will dry more quickly if you fill them with hot water. Empty when dry.
- In summer store them away from light and heat, preferably hanging up. Always store them empty.

Ironing board covers

Wash cotton covers like any other cotton material. Milium covers should be dry-cleaned.

Irons

The bases of modern irons are either aluminium or chrome-plated and do not tarnish but may acquire residues of various things which make them less smooth. It is essential to clean them immediately or ironing will be difficult and delicate fabrics may suffer.

- Disconnect the iron when you have finished ironing and before cleaning it.
- Let the iron cool in an upright position on its heel rest. Keep it like this when it is not in use during ironing sessions so you don't waste the steam.
- If the base has dried starch on it wipe it with a cloth wrung out in hot detergent solution.
- Remove melted nylon and other synthetic fibres by heating the iron then disconnecting it. While still hot wipe off the melted mess with a wooden (not plastic) spatula. Don't be tempted to use a sharp knife.
- From time to time rub the sole plate with beeswax and wipe off the surplus with a piece of kitchen tissue.
- If the opening of the sprinkler nozzle becomes blocked clear it with a fine sewing needle.

Ivory, bone and horn items

Dust frequently with a soft cloth. Wipe over with a mild detergent solution then with a clean damp cloth and dry carefully. Never immerse in liquid.

- Knives with ivory handles should not be soaked in water. Never put them in the dishwasher, just wash the blades in the washing-up bowl and dry them as quickly as possible.
- All ivory will yellow with age. Daylight will put off this process but don't leave items out in hot sun which will dry and crack it.

Jade objects

Jade is a silicate of calcium or magnesium. It usually only needs to be dusted but if necessary wash in a lukewarm mild soapsud solution. You can get a special detergent for cleaning jade and glass called Synperonic N (see addresses). If you wish to use this, use it very sparingly indeed, about 1 teaspoon to 4.5 litres (1 gallon) of water. Wash each piece separately in a plastic bowl.

Jewellery

Keep jewellery clean and store it carefully in separate boxes, not jumbled all together. Diamonds in particular can do a lot of damage to other pieces of jewellery and gold and platinum scratch easily. If you don't have enough boxes or compartments, wrap each piece separately in acid free tissue paper (from jewellers), or cotton wool.

• As a general rule it is cheap and quite satisfactory to wash jewellery with warm water and a mild detergent, using a soft toothbrush to get into the intricate parts. A little household ammonia in the water helps to loosen the dirt. Don't use very hot water which may expand the settings so that the stones fall out. Rinse in warm water and dry on a soft cloth with no loose threads that could catch on the setting.

• DO NOT use ammonia on pearls or coral.

• There are jewellery cleaning products on the market but they are, of course, more expensive than water and detergent. Follow the manufacturer's instructions. If in doubt, or for valuable and very old pieces seek professional advice first. The following hints concern specific kinds of jewellery:

Acrylic jewellery Sponge with lukewarm water and mild detergent. Wipe dry with a clean, damp cloth.

• If scratched, use a little metal polish.

Amber Wipe with a cloth wrung out in warm soapy water and dry at once. Water makes amber cloudy, so don't leave it in the solution.

• Clean grease marks with a bread ball or by wiping over with sweet almond oil.

Bead necklaces Re-string about once a year.

• Clean stones and beads with dry bicarbonate of soda on a soft brush.

Coral Treat exactly as for Pearls.

Costume jewellery Wash in warm water (hot water may crack the stones). Don't leave in the water for very long or the cement may come loose. If it does, use an epoxy resin to glue it back in.

Diamonds Take special care to keep diamonds clean so that the light will be reflected from each facet. Use an eyebrow brush or very soft toothbrush to loosen any dirt at the back of the setting.

• Diamonds may be boiled in a weak solution of soapsuds plus a few drops of ammonia. Place the object in a tea strainer or tie in a piece of muslin (like a bouquet garni) and dip it into the boiling liquid. Leave it there for just a moment. Remove and allow to cool. Dip it into an eggcupful of white spirit and lay it on paper tissues to dry.

- Don't, of course, boil diamonds if there are other stones in the setting.

Emeralds Washing may uncover hidden flaws and break the stones, so get them cleaned professionally.

Enamel Dust very occasionally with a watercolour paintbrush. Don't use water which can get between the layers and damage the piece.

Glass Wash in warm, detergenty water. Don't use hot or boiling water which may crack the glass. Don't leave in water for too long in case it softens the setting. Use a soft brush to get into the crevices.

- You can polish glass bracelets etc with a silver cloth or stainless-steel cleaner.
- Rub scratches with a chamois leather and jeweller's rouge, pressing lightly.

Gold and platinum Occasionally rub gently with a clean piece of chamois. Ordinary cloths may harbour bits of grit which could damage the metal.

- Treat gold plate with the tenderest care because the actual gold is only a very thin layer which may wear off with excessive rubbing.

Ivory Ivory absorbs liquid, swells up when wet and may crack so don't wash it in water. Clean with cotton wool dipped in whiting and methylated spirits.

- Give it a protective coating by rubbing it with a soft cloth dipped in sweet almond oil.
- You can slow up the yellowing process by keeping the ivory in the light. In the dark it will yellow much quicker.
- Bleach yellowed ivory by rubbing it with a cloth dipped in hydrogen peroxide and drying carefully with a soft cloth.
- Old ivory should be treated by a professional because you may ruin the patina.

Jet This is a sort of glossy black lignite (brown coal) also known as black amber. It was enjoyed by the Victorians who wore it as a symbol of mourning when Prince Albert died.

- Soft breadcrumbs can be used to clean pieces of jet. If it is not decorated with materials that water damages, then it can be washed as for Glass.

Opals Opals are very brittle so handle them carefully and don't expose them to extreme changes of temperature.

- Put them in a jar filled with powdered magnesia, shake it gently and then leave overnight. Brush the powder away with a soft watercolour or eyebrow brush.
- They may be washed in a warm water and mild detergent solution if not in a setting with materials that water damages.

Pearls Most natural pearls are found in oysters, though a few are found in clams. The oyster is sometimes attacked by a minute parasitic worm and builds the pearl round it to relieve the irritation. The pearl is built up in thin layers of mostly calcium carbonate. Pearls therefore dissolve in acid. Cultured pearls are made by putting a tiny bit of mother-of-pearl inside an oyster which duly covers it with pearl. Artificial pearls are made from hollow glass. The inside is covered with a special finish made from fish scales. If you want to test your pearls, real or cultured ones will feel rough if you draw them across your teeth. Artificial ones will feel smooth.

- Pearl necklaces should be restrung at least once a year or whenever they begin to get loose. Pearls are nearly always strung with a knot between each one, as are any valuable stones or beads, so that if the string breaks the whole lot won't scatter over the ground.
- To clean pearls, rub them gently with a clean soft chamois leather, taking care to rub between the beads to remove the film of dirt picked up from you and the atmosphere every time you wear them.
- Individual pearls may be washed in warm water and mild detergent (NEVER ammonia) but pearl necklaces should not be washed because the water may damage the thread.

Plaster and paste Dust frequently with a watercolour paintbrush. Wipe dirty marks with a clean cloth dipped in diluted ammonia. Washing will dissolve the paste.

Precious and semi-precious stones Rubies, amethysts, cairngorms, citrines, sapphires, turquoise and garnets can all be washed using detergent and water.

Silver Clean with a proprietary silver polish specially formulated for jewellery. Do not leave any polish on the silver because that will cause it to tarnish again more quickly and it will leave marks on your clothes.

- When cooking and washing up remove silver rings because contact with egg, fruit juices, olives, perfumes, salad dressing, salt, vinegar and so on all tarnish silver.

Wood Wipe wooden beads, bangles, brooches etc with a barely damp cloth. Don't immerse in water because it may stain or warp the wood.

- Polish with a little wax polish or rub in a little olive oil. Use tiny amounts and be sure to wipe off any excess or it will stain your clothes.

Lacquered goods (ornamental trays, boxes etc)

Wipe over with a barely damp cloth. About once a year apply the tiniest amount of furniture wax on a clean soft cloth and polish gently with a second cloth.

- Lacquered furniture should only ever need dusting.

Lampshades

Dust regularly using a duster, feather duster, or the dusting brush of a vacuum cleaner.

Fibreglass shades Wipe with a damp cloth.

Glass Shades Dust and wipe down with a cloth dipped in a solution of white vinegar and water.

Handpainted silk lampshades Dry-clean only. Water will damage any pattern and leave marks.

Kitchen lampshades get dirtier and greasier than others. Use a strong detergent – carpet detergent, say, in a strong solution. Or you can use white vinegar.

parchment shades Real parchment is made out of the skins of goats or sheep and should be conditioned occasionally with neat's foot oil or castor oil to prevent it drying out.

• Imitation parchment should be wiped with a damp cloth.

Plastic shades Wipe with a cloth wrung out in soapy water, then wipe with a cloth wrung out in clear water and dry with a soft cloth.

Raffia and straw Vacuum very frequently. They can be gently sponged with a just damp sponge from time to time.

Silk, nylon and rayon lampshades Wash them by hand, provided the shade is sewn and not glued to the frames and the trimmings are colourfast. Mix up a bowl of mild soap or detergent solution and dip the lampshade in and out. Rinse in the same way in tepid water. Stand the shade on a towel to dry, preferably in front of a fan heater because the quicker it dries, the less likely the frame is to rust.

• Silk, nylon or rayon which is glued to the frame should be dry-cleaned before it gets too dirty.

Luggage, leather

Carefully dust or wipe the luggage with a soft cloth wrung out in pure soapsuds or use saddle soap. Remove oily spots with a dry-cleaning solvent.

• Use neat's foot oil, lanolin or castor oil to keep leather luggage supple. Use after cleaning and apply it while the leather is still slightly damp. Rub it in with the fingers or a pad of soft cloth then leave it to soak into the leather. Neat's foot oil is difficult to polish afterwards, so if you want a polished finish use lanolin, castor oil or a half and half combination of the two instead.

• Use white petroleum jelly on white or light luggage.

Marble objects and surfaces

Polished marble should only be dusted or wiped with a soft, damp cloth. Antique marble should be dealt with by a professional.

- Really filthy marble can be cleaned with a cloth wrung out in mild detergent solution, but don't use this method more than once or the marble may discolour. Dry with a chamois leather so as not to leave streaks.
- Always wipe up spilled food, drinks, cosmetics etc quickly since they are liable to stain the marble.
- Clean marks with lemon juice or vinegar, but don't leave it on for more than a minute or two. Repeat if necessary. Little and often is the rule. Rinse and dry immediately.
- Organic stains from tea, coffee, cosmetics, tobacco, leaves, coloured paper and ink can be bleached with hydrogen peroxide. Dab it on with cotton wool and watch carefully to see when it is having an effect so that you don't leave it on too long.
- Deep oily and greasy stains can be absorbed by making a paste of dry-cleaning solvent and whiting, leaving it on the stain for several hours and then wiping if off. This is not guaranteed to remove stains but will help with some.
- Rust stains can be removed in the same way with a commercial rust remover added.
- Use proprietary marble cleaners for light scratches.

Mirrors

See Chapter 10.

Mother-of-pearl

This is the lining of sea shells. Clean it with soap and water. Don't use ammonia.

Musical boxes

Keep cylinder musical boxes out of direct sunlight and away from any form of heat or the glue that secures the mechanism may melt.
- Don't clean, oil or touch the mechanism. If necessary take it to a professional repairer.

Musical instruments

Keep musical instruments in their cases when they are not being played.
- Dust them with a clean, soft cloth and a very soft watercolour or eyebrow brush.
- Blow dust from the parts which are difficult to reach because of the strings etc.

Paintbrushes

Use the thinner for whatever paint you are using: water based paints need only water or detergent and water; lacquer needs a lacquer thinner or acetone; oil paints, varnishes and enamels need turpentine or white spirit; rubberised and synthetic resin paints need detergent and water; shellac needs methylated spirit, then soap and water. (Don't use white spirit to clean nylon brushes.) Pour a little of the solution onto the brush, work it in with gloved fingers and then paint as much as possible onto old newspaper. Some brushes may have to be left in thinner overnight. Or use a proprietary paintbrush cleaner which can deal with a number of different paints.

- Large brushes should be hung up by the handle. If you stand them on their heads, the hairs will be spread and distorted and if you stand them upside down the liquid flows back, weakening the mounting and making the hairs fall out. Drill a hole in the handle to hang the brush from. Or knock two nails into the wall about 25mm (1in) apart to hold each brush.
- Smaller brushes can be stored flat if not hung up. Wrap the damp paintbrush in a kitchen towel to stop the bristles from splaying out.
- Don't allow brushes to stand in any solution or the bristles will bend and become loose.
- Add a fabric conditioner to the final rinse to help keep brushes soft and pliable.

Parchment

See Lampshades.

Pianos

Pianos are given a specially hard shellac finish. Wipe with a soft cloth.
- Have the interior cleaned occasionally by a professional.
- Wipe the keys lengthways with a soft, slightly damp cloth, then dry with another soft cloth.
- Ivory keys will yellow with time. Sunshine helps to keep them white.

Pictures

Clean glass and frames with a cloth wrung out in water with a little white vinegar added. Don't get the water between the frame and the glass. Polish with paper towels or a chamois.
- Fly spots can be cleaned with cold tea.
- Apply wax polish to wooden picture frames if you wish or rub with a little olive oil.

Gilt frames Clean with a cloth moistened with a little dry-cleaning fluid.
Oil paintings Do not tamper with a painting you think may be

valuable. Get it dealt with by a professional. Local art shops or dealers may be able to offer advice. The cleaning techniques and materials used will depend on the type of paint and canvas.

- Dust the painting by lightly brushing with a cotton rag, a soft brush or a feather duster. Don't use soap, water, breadcrumbs or any of the other erasers sometimes recommended. A very fine film of cream furniture polish may brighten the surface. Make sure the canvas is supported from the back while you are cleaning the front. Most experts disapprove of any further cleaning being done by amateurs.

Watercolour paintings These are very difficult to clean so leave it to a professional. Erasers are too rough and crude but you can try a bread ball on a cheap watercolour.

Plastics

All plastics are easy to clean. Wipe them with a cloth wrung out in warm detergent solution.

Melamine Used to make plates, cups, tumblers, jugs, cutlery handles etc. It is strong, good looking, tasteless, non-toxic and doesn't smell. Boiling water will not damage it and it can be put in the dishwasher. However it does stain rather easily.

- Remove stubborn stains with a little toothpaste rubbed on with your finger or an old toothbrush. Don't use scouring powders or pads because melamine scratches easily. Sodium perborate is also usually effective on heavy stains.
- Bicarbonate of soda will often remove light stains.

Nylon plastic This is a very tough plastic. It is opaque or nearly white or tinted. It is not affected by freezing, is lightweight and rigid but slightly resilient. It is used for unbreakable tumblers, brushes and bristles.

- Nylon cutlery and crockery can be put in the dishwasher and nylon brushes can be boiled. (If you are not sure if they are nylon, don't boil them or put them in the dishwasher because acrylic and ordinary plastic won't stand up to such treatment.)
- Nylon utensils used for coffee or tea should be washed quickly before they become permanently stained. Don't use abrasives. Don't use them for cooking.

Playing cards

Paper cards should be wiped carefully with cotton wool moistened with white spirit and dried with clean tissue.

- Plastic cards only need to be wiped with a damp cloth.

Records and CDs

Clean records with a soft cloth moistened with a lukewarm mild

detergent solution. Then wipe with a cloth squeezed out in clear water. Wipe dry with a non-linty cotton or linen cloth.
- Clean CDs underneath with a cloth squeezed out in warm, detergenty water. Wipe dry with a non-linty cloth.

Roller blinds

Rub with a terry face flannel dipped in flour.

Shoe brushes

Soak in warm water and detergent solution containing a little household ammonia. Wash. Rinse well and dry with the head down.
- If the brush is caked with hardened shoe polish, soak it in a saucer of white spirit, rub it on newspaper or old rags and then wash it again.

Shoes and boots

Leather Remove surface dirt with a soft brush. If the shoes are muddy wait for the mud to dry and then remove it with a stiff brush. Any remaining mud can be removed with a soft damp cloth.
- Apply polish with a soft brush or shoe cream with a soft cloth.
- Buff up with a medium brush.
- Finish off by using a buffer (a small pad covered in velvet) for a high shine.

Patent leather Clean with a soft cloth wrung out in detergenty water. Buff up with a soft dry cloth. Wax will crack the leather but you can wipe a little milk over the surface and then buff up for extra shine.

Suede Brush with a special bristle, rubber or wire suede brush, working in a circular motion. Rub gently or you will damage the surface.

Slate

Wash slate worktops with mild detergent solution then apply a little lemon oil to make it lustrous. Wipe with a clean cloth after applying the oil to remove all excess.
- Instead of oil you can apply milk to give a lustre. Rub it down well afterwards with a clean cloth.
- Slate on worktops can be sealed with a special sealant which will keep the surface smooth, dark and dust free.

Soap dishes

Soak for a few minutes in a solution of 100g of washing-soda crystals dissolved in 3½ litres of very hot water (1 tablespoon to half a gallon). Scrub with a washing-up brush or a nail brush. Rinse and dry.

Spectacles

Wash occasionally with warm water and soap to remove accumulations of grease and oils from the skin and the atmosphere. Clean round the rims with a watercolour paintbrush. Give a final polish with a proprietary spectacle-cleaning paper or use tissues.

Sponges and loofahs

Sea sponges Wash in warm soapy water or detergent and water. If they have become slimy with soap, boil them in water and detergent. Allow to cool, squeeze out well and rinse. Don't bleach.
- Or soak overnight in salt water or bicarbonate of soda and water then wash in the dishwasher.

Plastic sponges These can be cleaned with a mild household ammonia solution of 25ml per litre of water (1 tablespoon per quart). This sometimes improves the colour and certainly disinfects them. Don't use strong bleaches or strong detergents. A weak solution of washing-up liquid and a weak solution of hydrogen peroxide should be OK.
- Synthetic or rubber sponge mops should be soaked before using because they are brittle when dry. Rinse well after use and hang up to dry naturally, away from direct heat or sunlight.

Sun lamps

Keep the reflectors brightly polished to reflect as much heat as possible. Use a proprietary impregnated wadding.

Taps

Keep chrome taps clean with a few drops of paraffin applied on a damp cloth. Paraffin dries quickly leaving no drips and the smell disappears almost at once. Metal polish is not necessary.
- Or use vinegar or lemon juice.

Teapots

Aluminium Fill with water and 100g (2 tablespoons) borax, boil and then wash as usual.

China Clean inside with a cloth moistened with water and dipped in bicarbonate of soda. Rinse in very hot water.

Chrome Clean inside with a cloth moistened with white vinegar and dipped in salt. Rinse in very hot water.

Silver Clean the inside with hot water and borax. Use 15g borax to 600ml water (1 teaspoon per pint). Leave for an hour then clean with a washing-up brush. Use a bottle brush for the spout. Rinse thoroughly. Clean the outside as you would for silver (see page 128).

Telephones

Dust telephones frequently. Wipe over from time to time with a damp cloth wrung out in detergent solution. Dry with a soft, clean cloth.

Televisions

Unplug before attempting to clean. Clean the screen with a cloth wrung out in mild detergent solution. The cloth should be barely damp. Dry with a clean, non-linty cloth.

- Don't use solvents, chemical cleaners or polishes which can damage the screen. Make sure dusters have no grit in them which could cause scratches.

Tortoiseshell

Clean with a paste made by moistening jeweller's rouge with one or two drops of olive oil. Rub on gently with a soft cloth. Leave for a few minutes then polish with a clean duster.

- Imitation tortoiseshell may be washed in warm soapy water then rinsed and dried.

Typewriters

Unplug electric typewriters before cleaning. Remove the platen and wipe it and the little rubber rollers that feed in the paper with dry cleaning solvent on a clean cloth. Brush out the dust and gunk from the platen holder.

- Clean the type with proprietary cleaning fluid or white spirit. Slip a piece of folded paper under the type bars and scrub the type with a stiff bristled typewriter brush or an old toothbrush. You can get spray-on cleaners or doughy cleaners for this job too. For golf ball and daisywheel typewriters follow the manufacturer's instructions.
- Move the carriage to the extreme left and put one drop of oil on the rails. Do not oil the type bars.

Vacuum flasks

Clean the inside with hot water and mild detergent or water and bicarbonate of soda. Use a bottle brush if necessary. Rinse thoroughly. Leave the top off until the flask is next used to make sure it grows no mould. Don't immerse the flask in water which might get between the interior and exterior or cause the metal casing to rust.

Vases

Wash the insides with warm water and detergent and if necessary use neat white vinegar to clean off the green gunge and hard water marks. Leave the vinegar in the vase for five or ten minutes, then clean with a bottle brush, rinse and dry. For narrow-necked vases see Glassware.

Venetian blinds

Wear a pair of cotton gloves and run the slats between your fingers and thumb. If the slats need more than just a dust dip them in detergent solution first.

VDUs

Clean as for a television set. Keep the cover on to prevent dust getting into the works.

Wooden bowls, boxes etc

Don't wash in water which will be absorbed and crack the wood. Wipe over with a barely damp cloth. Clean dust from carvings with a soft brush.

• Rub with a tiny quantity of olive oil and lemon juice if necessary. See also Jewellery.

13
A-Z of cleaning metals

Many metals tarnish easily, or can be easily scratched and become worn. Certain metals, such as copper (in roofs), bronze and pewter, may be admired for the patination they acquire with age, but most metals will benefit from regular care and attention and will last longer when protected from rust and corrosion.

Aluminium

Aluminium is made from naturally occurring alumina.

- Wash aluminium pans in mild detergent and water. Rinse in hot water and drain or dry with a soft tea-towel. Burned-on food should be left to soak then scraped off with a wooden spoon or spatula and cleaned with a soap-filled steel-wool pad. Aluminium cooking items can be washed in a dishwasher.
- Dull aluminium pans can be brightened by boiling up water in the pan with a tablespoon of white vinegar.
- Or add a teaspoon of cream of tartar to 600ml (1 pint) of water, bring to the boil and simmer for a couple of minutes.
- Don't keep food in an aluminium pan after cooking. Chemicals in the food may cause the metal to corrode and spoil the pan's looks as well as contaminating the food.
- Aluminium roasting tins need a lot of scouring to get rid of burned-on grease.

Brass

An alloy of copper and zinc.

- If very dirty wash first with a detergent solution.
- Traditionally brass was cleaned with oxalic acid and salt but oxalic acid is highly poisonous and so is not to be recommended. The right way is to use a proprietary metal polish, and follow the manufacturer's instructions.

- The lazy way is to buy lacquered brass which just needs an occasional wash in warm water and detergent. Unfortunately the lacquer often becomes damaged and the metal will then corrode under the remaining lacquer. All the lacquer will have to be removed in order to clean the brass before the item is re-lacquered. This is difficult to do and best done by a professional.
- The green way is to apply a paste of white vinegar and salt, or a piece of lemon. Leave on for five minutes or so, then remove and wash carefully. Dry then polish with an essential oil (from chemists or herbal shops) applied on a soft cloth.
- Very dirty objects such as fire tongs may have to be rubbed with steel wool or very fine emery cloth. Rub the metal up and down, not round and round. It will take some time. Rinse thoroughly in hot water and detergent and dry.
- Brass preserving pans should be cleaned inside with a paste of vinegar and kitchen salt. Wash and rinse thoroughly after cooking anything in them and dry well. Metal polish should never be used on the inside of a brass pan which is intended for cooking, but you can use it for the outside.
- Old brass pans which have not been used recently should be cleaned professionally if you intend to use them for cooking.

Bronze

An alloy of copper and tin.
- Bronze should never be washed or it might corrode irreparably. Don't touch the surface at all except to dust it lightly and even then very infrequently.
- Bronze corrodes easily forming a light green or sometimes even red, black or blue patina. This patination in antique bronzes is considered to be desirable. Antique bronzes require professional treatment.
- Nowadays solid bronze is often lacquered in the factory. Bronze with this sort of finish will only need dusting and, occasionally, a wipe with a damp cloth. If the lacquer cracks or peels it will have to be removed and the object re-lacquered.

Chromium

A soft, silvery metal which does not tarnish in air and can be highly polished.
- Wipe with a soft, damp cloth and polish with a dry one.
- Very dirty chrome can be washed with warm water and detergent. Dry thoroughly afterwards.
- The right way to clean chrome is to use a chrome cleaner from a car and bike accessory shop or hardware store.

- You can use a little paraffin applied on a damp cloth to clean fly-blown or greasy chrome.
- The green way is to use bicarbonate of soda on a damp cloth.

Cast iron

Wash in warm, soapy water, dry immediately, then coat with vegetable oil and keep in a dry place to prevent rust.
- Don't use harsh abrasives or metal scrapers.
- Don't run cold water into a hot pan.
- Don't store with the lid tightly on.

Copper

A lustrous red-brown metal.
- In air copper forms a greenish surface film which can cause nausea and vomiting if eaten. So copper pans must be kept scrupulously clean and should never have food left standing in them. Most modern copper pans are lined with chromium or tin. Some even have a non-stick surface.
- Do not cook food containing vinegar, lemon juice, rhubarb or other acids in an unlined copper pan as they will react with the metal and taint the food.
- Wash copper utensils and ornaments with water and detergent, rinse and dry well.
- Use a nylon scourer or nylon brush to clean burned-on food.
- Polish the exterior the right way with proprietary copper cleaner.
- The lazy way is to reduce the need to polish by having the copper lacquered.
- Polish the green way using vinegar or lemon juice and salt; or equal parts of salt, vinegar and flour; or buttermilk. Rinse at once and dry well.

Gold

See Jewellery, page 115.

Pewter

Pewter is an alloy of tin and various other metals, which may include lead, antimony, copper, bismuth and zinc.
- Ordinary pewter can be polished with a suitable proprietary metal polish or with whiting and a little household ammonia or a similar mild abrasive about two or three times a year.
- If kept in a humid atmosphere, pewter will quickly develop what's called a 'hume' with a grey film and tarnishing. Tarnish can be removed by immersing the item in solvent chemicals but only a specialist should do this.

Platinum

See Jewellery page 115.

Silver

A precious metal which is soft, white, lustrous and easily worked. Sterling silver contains at least 925 parts of silver to 75 parts of copper.

Silver needs constant care. It is best when used every day as constant use gives it a rich and mellow lustre. Nevertheless it will tarnish eventually. A damp, polluted or salty atmosphere will speed up the tarnishing. You can buy various bags, wraps and rolls of tarnish-inhibiting cloth and acid-free tissue paper to store silver in. These are available from jewellers. Don't store silver in plastic bags or self-stick plastic film and don't use rubber bands for securing the wrapping as rubber can corrode silver through several layers of cloth and the damage will be permanent.

- Wash silver as soon as you can after it has been used, in hot water and washing-up liquid. Rinse in hot water and dry at once.
- Wear cotton gloves when cleaning silver and treat the pieces gently. Old silver has often been worn leaf thin because it was cleaned with home-made, slightly abrasive products using whiting. Modern treatments should only remove the tarnish.
- Don't use silver cleaner on metals other than silver, gold or platinum.
- The right way to clean tarnished silver is to rub it with a proprietary silver polish using a soft cloth. There are paste, liquid or powder polishes, long-term polishes, dips and impregnated cloths and gloves.
- When polishing rub each piece briskly but not too hard, using even, firm, straight strokes.
- One way of cleaning silver-plated cutlery that is in daily use and for cleaning etched and embossed pieces is to use a proprietary dip product. If you can't get the object into the dip jar, dab it with cotton wool saturated in the solution. Don't leave items in the dip longer than necessary.
- Antique silver should be washed in warm water with a little Synperonic N added. (See page 142.) Dry thoroughly with muslin, paper towels or old, soft linen tea-towels. Do not use new linen cloths because the starch in them is too abrasive. When thoroughly dry, clean with a proprietary long-term silver cloth.
- Heavily tarnished antique silver should be treated with a proprietary silver dip applied with cotton-wool swabs, following the manufacturer's instructions. Dry with mutton cloth and polish with a long-term silver cloth. When dealing with a large object clean a small area at a time, rinsing off the silver dip before going

on to clean the next area. Don't use the same solution indefinitely because it becomes overcharged with silver which eventually gets deposited back on the surface as matt silver.

- Clean small objects with a brush specially made for cleaning silver. The bristles of toothbrushes or other household brushes are too rough and will scratch the surface.
- The lazy way of cleaning silver is to concoct your own electrolytic silver cleaner which is quick, simple, non-smelly, time saving and harmless but disapproved of by jewellers because it leaves the silver somewhat white and lustreless. Don't use it on antique silver or silverware with handles that may be fastened with cement.
  1 Fill a bowl with hot water.
  2 Dissolve a handful of washing soda in the water.
  3 Add a handful of silver milk bottle tops or aluminium foil (or use an aluminium pan instead of a bowl).
  4 Put in the silver making sure it is completely covered. Watch this brew seethe as the electro-chemical reaction removes the tarnish from the silver and deposits it on the aluminium. It should only take two or three minutes.

Stainless steel

Stainless steel is an iron alloy containing chromium. It is rust proof but salt and acids can cause pit marks if left in contact with it for too long.
- Wash stainless steel in hot detergent solution, rinse and dry.
- Corroded spots on cooking pans can be cleaned off with fine steel wool and a fine scouring powder. Polish with a soft cloth. Special stainless steel cleaners are available.
- Clean dulled stainless steel cutlery and tableware with a proprietory stainless steel polish. Don't use steel wool on tableware.

  Steel wool pads Those without soap often get rusty. To prevent them rusting, keep them in a cup of water with 3 tablespoons of bicarbonate of soda.

Tempered steel

Wash immediately after use and dry meticulously to prevent rusting. Scour with wire wool and scouring powder from time to time and keep knives well sharpened.

Wrought iron

Polish with liquid wax to prevent rust or treat with a rust inhibitor and then paint it with a paint specially made for iron.
- Remove rust spots with steel wool dipped in paraffin.

14
A-Z of household pests

One way to discourage pests is not to provide anything for them to eat or nest in. So wipe up crumbs after each meal, keep all food covered, do the washing-up regularly and don't leave uneaten cat or dog food on the floor. Fill cracks or holes in floors and walls. Don't allow stagnant water to collect near the house, disinfect your garbage bin, tie up all bags with garbage in them before putting them out of doors and keep the bin covered. Clean drains weekly with soda crystals washed down with boiling water.

This chapter suggests methods for dealing with specific unwanted pests in or near the house. If you are really plagued by pests such as rats or mice, or have a wasps' or bees' nest in the roof, you can call in the local health authority pest control officer who will probably charge a small fee, or a professional exterminator who will charge a larger one.

Always follow the manufacturer's instructions when using insecticides and store out of reach of children. Don't use near food (e.g. cover fruit bowls before spraying). If you get any on your skin, wash it off at once. On no account let any get near your mouth.

Ants

Follow their route march back to the nest and destroy it with a suitable insecticide, following instructions, or by pouring boiling water over it.

- Or deter them by blocking up the entrance hole with a piece of cotton wool soaked in paraffin. Then spray skirtings, beneath sinks and windowsills with insecticide. Take care pets and children can't get at it.
- Don't leave jams, sugars and fats where ants can find them.

Bedbugs

These lice-like insects hide during the day in cracks in walls and ceilings and appear at night to prey on you. They may be found in mattress seams, crevices in bedsteads, behind window and door frames, skirtings, picture mouldings, furniture, loose wallpaper and cracks in plaster.

- Use an insecticide containing malathion, lindane or pyrethrum and make sure it is suitable – too high a concentration of some insecticides is dangerous to humans. Spray it into all possible hiding places (bedsprings, frames, webbing and slats of beds) so they are thoroughly wet. Spray but don't soak the mattress, paying particular attention to seams and tufts. Spray skirtings and cracks in walls and floor boards.
- At any sign of another bedbug, spray the whole lot again with equal thoroughness. Better still, burn the mattress and get a new one.
- If in despair call out the local pest control officer.

Cockroaches

Big black beetles which lurk under refrigerators and other dark corners and appear at night to eat food, starch, fabrics and paper.

- Sprinkle infested areas with pyrethrum powder.
- If the infestation is bad, spray with a suitable insecticide and then sprinkle the powder, carefully blowing or fanning it into cracks and openings.

Fleas

Fleas will multiply readily in clean or squalid conditions if the house is warm enough. All pets who go outdoors will pick up fleas at some time. Infection with fleas may lead to dermatitis or tapeworm, and fleas may produce a violent allergic reaction in some dogs and cats.

- If an animal scratches a lot, check it over for fleas. Part the hair and look for the fleas scurrying away or for their dandruff-like droppings.
- Buy flea powders from a vet rather than a pet shop and always follow the manufacturer's instructions.
- Do not use flea powders intended for use on one sort of animal on another. Cats in particular can absorb a number of toxic substances through their skin, and both cats and dogs may be made ill by preparations wrongly applied. Don't let the powder come into contact with the animal's eyes or mouth.
- While treating your pet make sure you clean the house thoroughly at the same time; flea eggs can produce larvae in two to twelve days in warm conditions but may remain dormant for two months or much longer in cool temperatures. Vacuum

thoroughly especially in crevices, upholstery, skirting boards, cushions, and anything soft and warm. Burn the contents of the vacuum bag or seal it up in a plastic bag.
- Wash, burn or throw away the animal's bedding and use disposable bedding until the fleas have gone. Replace every few days.
- A bad infestation of fleas should be dealt with by the local pest control officer.

Flies

Flies can spread at least 30 different diseases to animals and people. They breed in garbage and rotting meat, especially in hot weather.
- Keep all food and garbage tightly covered. Keep dustbins clean. Make sure animal faeces are picked up or covered up.
- There are various suitable insecticides. All must be used strictly according to the manufacturer's instructions.
- Slow-release vaporized insect-killers are supposed to last six months and pose no health risk to humans or animals, but don't put them in rooms with the very old or the very young.
- Fly papers are effective and don't pollute the environment.

Mice

Mice are unhygienic and smelly. They eat biscuits, sugar and cheese, chew flexes and leave their droppings everywhere.
- Block any holes they may come in by (often under the sink and inside cupboards where the pipes run).
- Keep all food in sealed jars and tins.
- Keep all garbage tightly covered.
- Keep a cat. Often just the catty smell will keep mice at bay.
- Set traps. Peanut butter, cheese, bacon and cake make good bait. Put the traps at rightangles to the walls where you know mice visit and where children and pets can't get at them.
- Or use an anticoagulant poison specifically formulated for mice. Follow the instructions carefully. You may have to persevere for several weeks. Take care to put the poisons where they cannot be reached by the innocent.
- Other poisons are highly dangerous and should only be used by professionals.

Moths

Natural fibres are susceptible to moth larvae which can ruin clothes and curtains etc, by eating them. Man-made fibres are moth proof but, if blended with natural fibres, the material is still susceptible to damage. Clothes in daily use are not usually attacked but fabric

items which are stored are at risk, especially if they are not washed or cleaned before being put away.
- Clear out all cupboards and chests, vacuuming up dust, which moths breed in.
- Store clothes in polythene so moths can't get at them.
- Use spray-on moth deterrents. Or use moth deterrent sachets.
- The green way to keep moths at bay is to use camphor or turpentine. Alternatively place a mixture of cloves, cinammon, black pepper and orris root in small muslin bags and store these among the clothes. Or use dried orange peel or a few drops of lavender oil.

Rats

Rats will appear wherever there is food or somewhere to make a nest. Old rags left to rot in a shed will encourage them, so will open garbage cans or compost heaps containing too much food waste.
- Deal with the occasional rat by using poisoned bait. Some rats are developing an immunity to poisons and it may be sensible to use two different kinds: anticoagulants and multiple-dose poisons. Follow the directions very carefully and don't let children or pets get anywhere near them. Remove dead rats at once by placing them in a plastic bag, sealing it up and putting it in the garbage.
- If you are worried about a rat infestation, don't hesitate to contact your local health authority or to hire a professional.

Silver-fish

These are silvery insects about 10mm (half an inch) long, found on the floor in damp, cool places. They feed on sugar and starch and can damage books and rayon.
- Use a household insecticide, in spray or powder form, round doors, windows, skirtings, cupboards and pipes.

Spiders

Spiders are your friends. They will eat flies and other unfriendly insects and are harmless.

Woodworm

A woodworm infestation is recognisable by small round holes in woodwork or furniture, each about the size of a pin head and with sawdust spilling out. Woodworm may bore into furniture, wooden beams or floorboards.
- Treatment is best done by professionals.
- Small infestations can be treated with a DIY kit. Wear gloves to apply the product and keep it away from skin, eyes and mouth. Work outside or open windows and don't inhale the fumes.

15
A-Z of household products

A great many chemicals are used in proprietary household cleaning products, and there are many more which can be bought neat and used in a more diluted form which work just as well. There are also a few natural products which can do most of the household cleaning, which are safer, more environmentally sound and cheaper.

This guide is intended to be a quick reference to household cleaning substances, what they are made of, what they do and when it is appropriate to use them.

It is still not easy to get such information, and certainly not from labels on products. If in doubt write to the manufacturer for a list of contents.

Abrasives
Anything rough or gritty used to rub out stains or raise the nap of a fabric, such as whiting, pumice, scourers and sandpaper etc.

Absorbents
Anything which will soak up liquids (salt, fuller's earth, French chalk, talcum powder, silver sand, tissues etc).

Acetic acid (vinegar)
A colourless liquid used to brighten coloured fabrics by rinsing away alkaline residues caused by hard water which make coloured fabrics dull. Buy it from chemists, and dilute it in the proportions of 1 tablespoon to 4.5 litres (1 gallon) of water. Vinegar is a dilute, impure form of acetic acid but does many cleaning jobs very well.

Acetone
A solvent for animal and vegetable oils and for nail varnish. Also a

useful paint remover. Do not use on acetate fabrics as it will dissolve them. Available from chemists. Highly flammable.

Acids and alkalis

Acidity/alkalinity is measured by a number from 0 to 14 called pH. Pure water is pH 7 or neutral. Acidity is below 7, alkalinity above 7.

Acids Dissolve in water producing a sour solution (though many acids are far too poisonous to taste) and turn litmus paper red. The acids used in cleaning (acetic acid, citric acid) are usually mild. Water can be alkaline or acid. Too much alkali in the washing water can change the colours in fabrics. Acids can counteract this colour change.

Alkalis (ammonia, caustic soda, and other soda compounds) Soluble in water. Alkaline water tastes bitter, feels slippery and turns litmus paper blue. Alkalis neutralise acids, will rot animal and vegetable substances (wool and silk or rayon for instance) and will change colours in many dyes.

Mild alkali soaps have a pH of 8–10. Soapless detergents can have a pH of almost 7 (neutral). Strong alkali washing powders may have a Ph of 10–11 and are mainly used for cotton and linen. Wool, silk, rayon and coloured fabrics need a pH of between 7 and 8.

Air fresheners and air purifiers

Some conceal odours with their own. Others actually destroy smells by reacting with them chemically. There are aerosol air fresheners, some which refresh from a wick and some which hang inside the lavatory pan and some which release their odour gradually when opened. A clean home should not need air fresheners or purifiers but they may be useful to counteract the smell if someone's been sick or the cat has been caught short indoors. If you want to be green don't use the aerosols.

• Air purifiers contain an antiseptic ingredient such as triethylene glycol.

Alcohols (including ethanol, methylated spirit, surgical spirit, methanol or wood alcohol, isopropyl alcohol)

A large class of organic chemicals of which the most important is ethanol, produced by yeast during the fermentation of sugar. A 70% solution of ethanol in water is a good disinfectant. It is useful in cleaning because it dissolves grease and evaporates rapidly. Useful for cleaning glass.

Alkalis

See Acids and alkalis.

Ammonia

A colourless gas with a pungent, penetrating odour. Dissolves readily in water to form ammonium hydroxide, which is an alkali and grease solvent. Buy household ammonia which is ammonia solution specially prepared for domestic use; cloudy ammonia is household ammonia with a little soap added.

- Do not use ammonia on silk, wool, aluminium or sisal.
- Wear gloves while using ammonia. Don't sniff the liquid and handle with caution. If you get any on the skin or near the eyes, wash off with plenty of cold water. Then use a dilute acid (1 level teaspoon boric acid to 600 ml/1 pint water) for the eyes and a weaker one (1 tablespoon to 600 ml/1 pint water) for the skin.
- Many metal polishes contain ammonium hydroxide which removes any metal oxides, especially of copper.

Amyl acetate

A solvent for celluloid and cellulose paint and nail varnish. Available from chemists. It smells of peardrops. Should be safe on acetate fabrics unless what is spilled on them contained acetone and the fabric is already damaged. Inflammable and toxic; don't breathe fumes and keep windows open when using.

Bathroom and kitchen cleaners

Various different types including cream cleaners and liquid cleaners. Some may be slightly abrasive. Kitchen cleaners will contain more alkali, bathroom cleaners more acid.

Bicarbonate of soda

See Sodium bicarbonate.

Beeswax

Obtained from honeycombs. Sold in 275 g (10 oz) blocks in chemists and hardware shops. Used in some furniture polishes.

- Make your own furniture polish with 30 g (1 oz) beeswax to 140 ml (¼ pint) turpentine. Scrape the beeswax into the turpentine and leave to dissolve for several days. Shake well before using.

Blacklead (also known as graphite and plumbago)

Used for blacking grates etc. It is a natural crystalline form of carbon and nothing to do with lead. Modern versions are available in tubes.

Blue or washing blue

This is a water-soluble blue dye. A tiny bit in the wash will make yellowish fabrics look white. Many washing powders contain small amounts of blue anyway. But there are cheap powder blues and liquid blues available from supermarkets should you want to use them.

Borax

A white crystalline alkali mineral salt slightly soluble in water. Used as a water softener in laundry, bath and shampoo products, and as an antiseptic. It loosens dirt and grease and retards the growth of many moulds and bacteria.

Bran

The inner husks of corn sifted from flour. Use it as an absorbent and a dry shampoo for fur coats and hats and shaggy, non-washable fabrics.

Builders

Substances added to laundry detergents to increase cleaning efficiency. They include sodium carbonate, borax, sodium silicate and sodium phosphates. 'Built' soaps should not be used for washing the face or hands or washing delicate fabrics.

Carbolic acid (phenol)

A weak acid and a powerful disinfectant. Used in general disinfectants for cleaning floors, drains and WCs and in timber preservatives. Cresols are similar. The efficiency of a disinfectant is measured against phenol which is used as a standard comparison.

Carbon tetrachloride

This has no place nowadays in the household. It is extremely poisonous.

Castor oil

Comes from the bean of the castor oil plant. Good leather conditioner, especially for polished leather.

Caustic soda (lye, or sodium hydrate, or sodium hydroxide)

A strong alkali used for cleaning ovens and bad stains on baths and basins. Can be bought as a jelly or as a stick cleaner or a liquid. Used in many lavatory cleaners and for unblocking drains.
- Do not use it to clear kitchen sink outlets, because it could combine with grease to form a hard soap which will block the drain completely. Use washing soda and boiling water instead.
- Caustic soda will burn through cloth, enamel, bristle brushes, rubber gloves and damage aluminium. When using caustic soda,

follow the manufacturer's instructions carefully. Don't get it on the skin or near the eyes. If you do, wash with lots of cold water.

Chlorine bleach

Sodium hypochlorite is a chlorine compound used in household bleaches. It has a characteristic and suffocating smell. Useful for bleaching white cottons, linens and synthetics but do not use on silk, wool, mohair, leather, elasticated drip-dry or other resin-treated fabrics. Always test a sample of the fabric first. Even cotton and linen will weaken if left in the solution too long. Follow manufacturer's instructions.

- Chlorine bleach will remove stains from baths, sinks, enamelware, tiles and woodwork. Use about 2 tablespoons to 600ml (1 pint) water. If necessary soak a pad of cotton wool or tissues in the solution and leave it on the stain for five minutes or so.
- If you use bleach as a lavatory cleaner do not use other cleaners at the same time. Chlorine and ammonia and other preparations used in lavatory cleaners produce a chemical reaction and a poisonous gas which can be very dangerous.
- Chlorine bleach can lose its effectiveness if stored for too long.

Citric acid (lemon juice)

A mild acid which can be used to counteract alkali stains, remove hard water scale, clean brass etc.

Cresols

Derivatives of phenol (see Carbolic acid) found in coal tar. Powerful disinfectant. Used in lavatory cleaners and general disinfectants.

Descaling products

Used for removing fur or scale caused by minerals in hard water. Kettles, hot water tanks, steam irons and water pipes are all likely to get furred up if you live in a hard-water area. Proprietary descalers are available from hardware stores. Follow the manufacturer's instructions carefully. Some descalers can be used on their own, others have to be used with household ammonia.

- It's not necessary to buy special preparations though. A tablespoon of borax to a kettleful of water will descale the kettle and so will vinegar (see page 71).

Detergents

Traditionally the word detergent describes any substance that cleans surfaces or removes dirt. Nowadays soap-based detergents are called soap and synthetic detergents are called detergents. Most synthetic detergents are based on petroleum by-products. Additives or builders of various kinds are added to many detergents to make them clean better and to prevent dirt being redeposited on the fibres. Perfumes and bleaches are also included. An important feature of detergents is their degree of alkalinity (see Acids and alkalis). Most household detergents are neutral as this does little damage to surfaces or skin, but the higher the pH value of a detergent, the better it is at removing dirt.

- Synthetic detergents dissolve easily in hot or cold water and are effective in hard water without the use of water softeners. They do not create scum and don't leave a film on washed surfaces or in bowls or buckets.
- Detergents vary in strength and blueness etc. Too much detergent will eventually make clothes greyish and coloured clothes dull because of the added blue. Other additives may include: a cellulose dirt-suspending agent, builders (mainly phosphates), suds stabilisers, metal protector to prevent corrosion of aluminium, oxygen bleach (sodium perborate, which won't work at low temperatures), enzymes, fluorescent whitening agents (which only work properly on thoroughly clean fibres), colouring and perfume. Heavy duty detergents have the most additives.
- Biological (enzyme) detergent must be used with cool water. The enzymes need time to work and are best used as a pre-wash treatment. Soaking in ordinary detergent is safer and probably just as effective.
- Greener detergents are those which have the fewest, if any, phosphates, bleaching agents, enzymes and perfumes.

Disinfectants

Used to kill or check germs and bacteria on surfaces (as opposed to antiseptics which are used in or on the body).

The first disinfectants used in surgery were carbolic acid solutions. Then cresols and phenols were found to be more effective and in 1930 chloroxylenol was evolved. The main types of disinfectants used in homes today are: chlorine bleaches, hydrogen peroxide, phenol, cresol, chloroxylenol, quaternary ammonium compounds and triethylene glycol, used in antiseptic air purifiers.

Enzymes

See Detergents.

Ether

A solvent which dissolves animal oils and fats. Highly flammable. Not recommended for general use.

Ethyl alcohol
See Alcohols.

Fabric conditioners
Sometimes called fabric softeners or fabric retexturisers. Used in laundry rinsing water to make textiles soft and fluffy and less likely to crease and to help reduce static electricity especially in synthetic fibres. They must be used with each wash.
• Try to find non-perfumed ones.

Fluorocarbons
Wide range of synthetic chemicals used in commercial dry-cleaning solvents. They are in the process of being withdrawn because their manufacture damages the ozone layer but will probably be with us for another ten years.

French chalk (taylor's chalk, soapstone or steatite)
A compact kind of talc with a soapy feel. Powdered French chalk can be used as an absorbent for soaking up fresh grease stains from fabrics. It is quite harmless to all fabrics and will not leave a mark.

Fuller's earth
Clay mineral used as an absorbent, to remove grease from unwashable fabrics.

Germicide
Anything that kills bacteria, mould and yeast.

Hydrochloric acid (spirits of salts)
A colourless liquid with a strong smell. A solution of hydrochloric acid in water is called muriatic acid and is used to clean down new bricks and tiles. The solution is dangerous, will damage skin, woodwork and fabric and should be used only by professionals.

Hydrogen peroxide
A disinfectant and a bleach available from chemists in a dilute solution (usually in 20 parts its own volume of water) which should be further diluted for use at home. Will damage fabric and skin if left in contact too long or used in too strong a solution.

Isopropyl alcohol
A solvent sometimes used instead of methylated spirit for dissolving lacquer, varnish, French polish and removing ball-point pen marks.

Javelle water

Solution of sodium hypochlorite in water. (See Chlorine bleach.)

Lanolin

A sticky yellow wax obtained from sheep fleece. It is mainly a mixture of fatty acids, alcohols and cholesterol. Can be used as a conditioner for leather.

Laundry solvents

Bars of soap-like detergent and solvent which can be rubbed onto collars, cuffs and stains before laundering a garment and onto carpets to clean stained areas.

Lavatory cleaners

Powder cleaners, which are based on sodium acid sulphate, should never be used on any surface other than the loo pan as they are corrosive.
- Bleach is often used as a cheap cleaner and disinfectant for lavatory pans.
- Caustic soda is also used in lavatory cleaners.
- Don't use two different lavatory cleaners together because the result may be toxic or explosive or both.
- For everyday cleaning a vinegar and water solution can be quite satisfactory for the lavatory (see page 75).

Lemon juice

Paraffin oil (mineral oil) with a little oil of lemon in it.

Linseed oil

An oil from common flax seeds with practically no taste or smell. Used for making oil paints, varnishes and furniture polishes and for oiling natural wood. Boiled linseed oil is darker and has a strong, characteristic smell. Highly flammable.

Lye

Any strong alkali used for making soap and for various cleaning operations. Used in many lavatory cleaners and for unblocking drains. Common household lye is usually sodium hydroxide (caustic soda). It is highly dangerous and can cause severe external as well as internal poisoning. It will burn through cloth, enamel surfaces, bristle brushes, rubber gloves and damage some metals including aluminium.

Lysol

A very strong and poisonous disinfectant which is a solution of cresols in soap.

Methanol (methyl alcohol, wood alcohol)

This is one of the things put into ethanol to make it undrinkable (when it becomes methylated spirits).

Methylated spirits (denatured spirits)

Ethanol with additives including dye and methanol. Dissolves essential oils, castor oil, shellac and certain dyes, ball-point pen ink, iodine, grass stains and some medicines. Useful for cleaning mirrors and glass objects. Highly flammable, poisonous.

Milton

Brand name for a bleach and disinfectant used specially for disinfecting nappies and babies' bottles.

Moth proofers

Moth proofing crystals made of paradichlorobenzene are available in small bags to keep moths out of clothes storage cupboards and trunks. Traditional moth balls are made of napthalene and smell very strong.
- The green way to deter moths is to put any or all of the following in a muslin bag and place it among the clothes: camphor, lavender, cloves, cinnamon, black pepper and orris root.

Muriatic acid

See Hydrochloric acid.

Naptha

Made from coal tar. Used as a rubber solvent and a solvent for certain greasy stains and in some paints, varnishes and wax polishes. It is one of the things added to methylated spirits to make it undrinkable. Highly flammable. Don't store at home.

Neat's foot oil

Amber coloured oil from the feet of cows and similar animals. Excellent leather conditioner and protector (but not cleaner). Clean the leather with saddle soap first then rub the oil in with the finger tips. Don't use on shiny surfaces because it is difficult to polish up afterwards. From chemists, shoe shops, hardware shops and some haberdashery departments.

Neutralisers

Neutralisation is something done to remove acid or alkaline residues from clothes after washing. Acetic acid (or white vinegar) will rinse away alkaline residues caused by soap or the deposits left by soap reacting with calcium in hard water, which make coloured fabrics look dull. Ammonia rinses remove acidic residues after using sodium hypochlorite bleaches or after using an acid stain remover.

Oven cleaners

The caustic used for cleaning ovens is very strongly alkaline. Wear gloves and don't let it touch any aluminium pans.

Oxalic acid

One of the strongest organic acids. Found in wood sorrel (oxalis) and rhubarb leaves. Highly poisonous. Wear protective gloves. It is used for stain removal and cleaning brassware and also as a bleach and stain remover especially for ink and rust stains. Dissolve 1 teaspoon of oxalic crystals in 300 ml (half a pint) of warm water in a glass or china dish. Test before using on nylon or rayon. Rinse well with water.

Paraffins

A group of hydrocarbons obtained from petroleum. Paraffin wax is used in some furniture polishes, in cold creams and in hair preparations. Liquid paraffins are burned in paraffin stoves and can be useful for removing rust from bicycle and motorcar parts, ancient screws, nuts and bolts etc. It is poisonous and flammable.

Perchloroethylene

A non-flammable solvent used in most professional dry-cleaning machines.

Petroleum jelly

The semi-solid form of mineral oil (distilled from crude oil). Used to lubricate grass stains and other marks, making them easier to remove.

Potassium hydrogen oxalate (salts of lemon)

Used as an iron stain remover. Poisonous. Available from chemists.

Pumice

Frothy stones of lava from volcanoes. Used for smoothing and cleaning. Powdered pumice is used as an abrasive.

Rottenstone (tripoli)

Used in metal polishes. Mixed with linseed oil it will get rid of white spots on polished wooden furniture. Apply lightly with a soft clean cloth along the grain of the wood.

Rouge

Jeweller's rouge is a red powder made of ferric oxide. It is used for cleaning and polishing metals, silver, glass, gemstones etc. Silver polishing cloths are often impregnated with rouge.

Rust removers and inhibitors

Removers and inhibitors are sometimes incorporated in one product.
- Rust on clothes can be treated with oxalic acid or a proprietary dye remover. Slight stains may come out with lemon juice.
- Use wire wool pads to remove rust from kitchen utensils.
- Use a proprietary remover from car accessory shops or hardware shops for outdoor tools, bicycles and cars.

Saddle soap

A special soap used for cleaning leather. Use it on all polished leathers.

Salt (sodium chloride)

Neutral. May be used as an absorbent for liquid stains on carpets. May be used as an absorbent together with olive oil for white ring stains on polished wood furniture.

Salts of lemon

See Potassium hydrogen oxalate.

Silicones

Derived from the mineral silica. They resist water, electricity, weathering, chemicals and don't react to heat or cold. Used in water-proofed clothing, barrier hand creams and in small amounts in many polishes, not just for protection but because they help the product to spread. Also included in metal polishes.

Silver sand

Clean, fine sand. Used as an absorbent and an abrasive. From ironmongers or domestic stores in small quantities; nurserymen or garden suppliers for sand-pit or fire-bucket quantities.

Soap

Manufactured from animal fats such as mutton fat, or tallow and olive or palm-kernel vegetable oils and caustic soda. Builders are often added to household bar soaps and laundry soaps. These include sodium carbonate, borax, water-glass and sodium phosphates. Don't use such soaps for washing the body.

• A soap is said to be neutral when there is a correct balance between fat and soda. To much soap will spoil a wash.

Sodium bicarbonate (bicarbonate of soda, baking powder)

White powder used as a mild alkali for laundry work. Will remove stains from china, glass, tiles, false teeth and the refrigerator. You can also wash jewellery in it. Non-poisonous.

Sodium carbonate (washing soda, soda ash, sal soda)

Crystalline powder or crystals. Medium alkali for laundry work. Water softener, varnish remover, silver tarnish remover. Useful for cleaning and clearing drains. Do not use on aluminium, silk, wool, sisal or vinyl flooring. Wear gloves when using or apply a greasy hand cream after contact.

Sodium hexametaphosphate

A neutral water softener that is more gentle than washing soda. Easily dissolved. Expensive.

Sodium hydroxide (sodium hydrate, caustic soda, lye)

A very strong alkali. Used in the manufacture of soap, as a grease remover for ovens, sinks and drains and as a paint remover. Poisonous and can cause bad skin burns. (See also Caustic Soda.)

Sodium hypochlorite (javelle water, labarraque solution)

Chlorine or household bleach. Made of washing soda and chloride of lime with water. (See also Chlorine Bleach.)

Sodium hyposulphite

Colour remover useful for bleaching and stain removal.

Sodium perborate

A soft bleach suitable for all fabrics but don't use a hot solution on heat-sensitive fabrics such as wool, silk or synthetics.

• When using proprietary sodium perborate preparations follow the manufacturer's directions. Pure sodium perborate crystals can be bought from chemists. Use china or glass and not metal containers to mix the bleach in.

Sodium sesquicarbonate

A powdery alkaline water softener. A combination of washing soda and bicarbonate of soda. Dissolves easily. More effective and milder than washing soda. Cheaper than sodium hexametaphosphate.

Sodium silicate (water glass)
Used for preserving eggs and sometimes as a paint stain remover and as a builder in soaps.

Sodium thiosulphate (sodium hyposulphite, 'hypo')
Can be used to remove chlorine and iodine stains on all fibres. Won't affect colours.

Solvent
A substance used to dissolve another substance. In this book solvent means specifically a liquid which will dissolve the greasy dirt from fabrics. Solvents include perchloroethylene, trichloroethane and proprietary household spot removers. Methylated spirit, acetone, amyl acetate, turpentine, isopropyl alcohol and ether are all solvents.

Starch
Usually made from cereals and used to stiffen fabrics and give them body.

Stove polish
See Blacklead.

Surgical spirit
Methylated spirit with small amounts of castor oil and oil of wintergreen added. Used among other things as a solvent. Flammable and toxic.

Synperonic N
A neutral detergent used for cleaning very delicate glass and china and antique silver.

Talc
A soft, pliable, greasy, silvery-white powdery mineral. Used as an absorbent.

Teak oil
A treatment for natural teak, and other untreated woods, sometimes used instead of polish.

Trichloroethane

A non-flammable and not very toxic solvent used in many proprietary grease stain removers.

Trichloroethylene

Non-flammable solvent used mainly for industrial metal-degreasing applications.

Tripoli

See Rottenstone.

Trisodium phosphate

Similar to washing soda. Sold as TSP in decorating shops for cleaning paint. Use it to clean glazed and unglazed ceramic tiles and most paints. It will make enamel paint dull.

Turpentine

A balsam made from pine trees. Used as a solvent in some paints, varnishes and waxes. Always use real turpentine when specified as there is no real substitute.

Vaseline

Trade name for a specific petroleum jelly.

Washing soda

See Sodium carbonate.

Water

Water is the commonest, cheapest cleaner available. It's always worth treating a non-greasy stain with lots of clear water before trying other cleaners. Soft water will produce a lather which lasts five minutes when mixed with soap. Hard water doesn't lather easily because of certain salts it has collected when it ran over rocks. Hard water forms a sort of curd with soap, giving a grey look to textiles and damaging the texture. It also appears as a tide line on the bath. Rinsing in water will not get rid of it, but white vinegar can be used to give an acid rinse. Rainwater is soft and good for washing hair and rinsing clothes. Collect it in a water butt.

Water softeners

If your water is hard use soapless detergents rather than soap. Washing soda, sodium hexametaphosphate or sodium sesquicarbonate are all suitable for softening water and the last two are ingredients in many laundry washing-powders and bath salts.
- Plumbed-in water softeners can be fitted into the main water system of a house. Installing such a system is expensive but in

areas where the water is very hard it will make washing and cleaning much easier and prevent the furring up of water cisterns and pipes.

Wax

Natural waxes are hard non-greasy solids which do not leave grease marks on paper as other fats do. They are obtained from either plant or animal sources. Waxes are used in various ways for polishing and protecting furniture, cars, shoes, floors etc. There are also synthetic waxes for use in polishing and waterproofing. Paste waxes are made of wax and white spirit. The spirit evaporates leaving a thin film of wax. Liquid waxes are thin creams of wax with an emulsifying agent and water. Silicones may be added to make these polishes spread more easily and help to make them more water-repellent.

• Natural waxes include *carnauba*, which is made from the leaves of a Brazilian palm and is very hard. It is used for furniture, floors, shoes, cars and toughening other soft waxes and beeswax.

White spirit

Colourless solvent made from a mixture of mineral oils. Used as a thinner for paints, a general purpose grease and stain remover and in the manufacture of polish. It helps the polish to spread but evaporates quickly leaving a hard, smooth surface. It is flammable, toxic and will dry out the natural oils from your hands so use a greasy hand cream after using it. If you wear rubber gloves, wash them afterwards.

White vinegar

See Acetic acid.

Whiting

Finely ground chalk, free from impurities, used as an abrasive and a colouring in cleaning powder, polishes and putty. There are various grades available.

Addresses

Advisory

Association of British Launderers and Cleaners:
No longer exists under this name. See Textile Services Association.

British Man-made Fibres Federation and **British Textiles Federation**
24 Buckingham Gate, London SW1E 6LB. Tel: 071–491 9704 (BMMFF);
071–491 9702 (BTF).
Booklet *Guide to Man-made Fibres* and statistics, educational information packs and videos.

British Standards Institution (BSI)
Enquiries: Linford Road, Milton Keynes MK14 6LE. Tel: 0908 221166 (queuing system).
Information on British Standards for textiles and clothing.

Consumer's Association
2 Marylebone Road, London NW1. Tel: 071–486 5544.
Members receive monthly copies of *Which?* magazine and can ask for advice when confronted with consumer problems.

Good Housekeeping Institute
National Magazine House, 72 Broadwick Street, London W1V 2BP. Tel: 071–439 5000.
Leaflets and advice on various aspects of cleaning.

Dry Cleaning Information Bureau (DIB) and **Laundry Information Bureau (LIB)**
7 Churchill Court, 58 Station Road, North Harrow HA2 7SA. Tel: 081–863 8658.
Will give names of specialist cleaners in your area who are members of the organisation.

Dylon International Ltd
Worsley Bridge Road, Lower Sydenham, London SE26 5HD. Tel: 081–650 4801.
Has a consumer help line which will advise on dyeing and removing dyes and stains with Dylon products.

Friends of the Earth
Head Office: 26–28 Underwood Street, London N1 7JQ. Tel: 071–490 1555.
Campaigning organisation for the environment. Network of local groups. Publications on 'green' issues.

Home Laundering Consultative Council (HLCC)
British Apparel and Textiles Centre, 7 Swallow Place, London W1R 7AA. Tel: 071–408 0020 (Tuesdays and Thursdays only).
The UK National Care Labelling Authority and a voluntary membership organisation for all

branches of the textile and laundry industry. Its aims are to formulate useful consumer advice on textile care, to establish agreed terminology and definitions relating to home laundering advice, to provide nationally and internationally a public voice for the interested parties concerned in matters of home laundering and to develop and promote a complete international textile care labelling scheme. Will answer queries on the Care Labelling Code and have publications on testing for washability, dry-cleanability, tumble drying etc and an educational service for schools and higher education.

Laundry Information Bureau (LIB)
See Dry Cleaning Information Bureau.

Lever Bros Consumer Advice Service
Lever House, 3 St. James's Road, Kingston-upon-Thames, Surrey KT1 2BA.
Tel: 081–541 8200.
Will advise on all aspects of laundering, with a bias towards their own products.

National Association of Citizens' Advice Bureaux
Head Office: 136–144 City Road, London EC1Y 2QN. Tel: 071–251 2000
Look in Yellow Pages for local branch. For advice and information on legal and consumer problems.

National Association of the Launderette Industry
South Lodge, 79 Glen Eyre Road, Southampton SO2 3NN
Will arbitrate in disputes between members of the public and any of their members. Please make a note of the exact address of any launderette you are in dispute with.

National Carpet Cleaners Association
126 New Walk, De Montfort Street, Leicester LE1 7JA. Tel: 0533 554352
Runs courses for members or carpet cleaning businesses who wish to become members. Will give names of local members. Code of practice.

Office of Fair Trading
Room 306, Field House, Breams Buildings, London EC4A 1PR. Tel: 071–242 2858 (general enquiries); 071–269 8889 (schools' liaison service).
Government funded organisation involved in negotiating various codes of practice. Will arbitrate on complaints submitted through local authority Trading Standards office. Has free leaflets on various aspects of fair trading.

Textile Services Association
7 Church Hill Court, 58 Station Road, North Harrow, Middlesex HA2 7SA.
Trade association for launderers and dry cleaners. Will give addresses of specialist cleaners in your area who are members of the association and will also help with complaints about members. Publish and sell booklet called *Fabric and Garment Care*. Confusingly, members carry ABLC symbol on their premises because the TSA used to be called the Association of British Launderers and Cleaners.

WIRE Technology Group Ltd
WIRE House, West Park Ring Road, Leeds LS16 6QL
Information on caring for and cleaning wool.

Vitreous Enamel Development Council (VEDC)
New House, High Street, Ticehurst, Wadhurst, Sussex TN5 7AL. Tel: 0379 650340
Tests materials for vitreous enamel and will supply an up-to-date list of safe cleaners.

Suppliers and Services

Amari Plastics Ltd
Head Office (for address of nearest of 12 branches): 24–30 Baker Street, Holmes House, Weybridge, Surrey KT13 8AV. Tel: 0932 54803.
Sell an anti-static liquid spray for acrylics.

Archival Aids
Unit 29, Trentland Industrial Estate, Castle Donnington, Derbyshire DEX 2NP.
Suppliers of Synperonic N.

Connolly Bros (Curriers) Ltd
Wandle Bank, Wimbledon, London SW19 1DW. Tel: 081–542 5251.
Suppliers of Connolly's Hide Food. Will advise. Ask for Renovation Department.

Ecover
Mouse Land, Steyning, West Sussex BN44 3DG.
Manufacturers of a range of cleaning and laundering products which are ecologically green and not tested on animals. Will give names of stockists.

Faith Products Ltd
Unit 5, Bury Industrial Estate, Kay Street, Bury, Lancashire BL9 6BU. Tel: 061–764 2555.
Manufacturers of Clear Spring green products including a washing-up liquid, dishwasher liquid and rinse aid. Will give address of nearest stockist.

G. E. Holloway & Son, (Engineering) Ltd
12 Carlisle Road, Colindale, London NW9 0HL. Tel: 081–200 0066.
Will supply address of your nearest stockist of Holloway's Chewing Gum Remover, spotting kit (four bottles for different stains) and rust remover (good for rust on carpets caused by leaking radiators).

The National Trust (Enterprises) Ltd
PO Box 101, Western Way, Melksham, Wiltshire SN12 8EA. Tel: 0225 705676.
Sells Banister brushes, blacklead brushes, radiator brushes and other specialist brushes for special furniture.

Pilgrim Payne & Co Ltd
290–294 Latimer Road, London W10 6QU. Tel: 081–960 5656.
Specialise in dry-cleaning furnishings, tapestries and fine carpets. Has a delivery postal service.

Parker Pen Company Ltd
Service Department, PO Box 6, Newhaven, Sussex BN9 0AX. Tel: 0273 513233.
Stain removal instructions for all Parker Pen inks.

Picreator Enterprises Ltd
44 Park View Gardens, Hendon, London NW4 2PN. Tel: 081–202 8972.
Manufacturers of Renaissance Wax furniture polish. Will give names of stockists and operate a mail order service.

Royal School of Needlework
Apartment 38, Hampton Court Palace, East Molesy, Surrey KT8 9AU. Tel: 081–943 1432.
Will clean and repair needlepoint and other embroidery. Ring for appointment because the security department at Hampton Court won't accept authorised visitors.

Index